Feminist Pillar of Fire

Alma begins a decade of involvement with the Ku Klux Klan and the National Woman's Party, c. 1920

Feminist Pillar of Fire

THE LIFE OF ALMA WHITE

Susie Cunningham Stanley

The Pilgrim Press
Cleveland, Ohio

The Pilgrim Press, Cleveland, Ohio 44115
© 1993 by The Pilgrim Press

Printed in the United States of America
The paper used in this publication is acid free and meets the
minimum requirements of American National Standard for
Information Sciences-Permanence of Paper for Printed
Library Materials, ANSI Z39.48-1984

98 97 96 95 94 93   5 4 3 2 1

Library of Congress Cataloging-in-Publication Data

Stanley, Susie Cunningham,   1948–
    Feminist Pillar of Fire   :   the life of Alma White   /   Susie
Cunningham Stanley.
        p.   cm.
    Includes bibliographical references and index.
    ISBN 0-8298-0950-3 (alk. paper)
    1. White, Alma, b. 1862.   2. Pillar of Fire (Religious sect)—
History.   3. Women evangelists—United States—Biography.
4. Feminism—Religious aspects—Christianity—History.   I. Title.
BX8795.P5S734   1993
289.9—dc20
    [B]   92-43013
                                                                            CIP

To Mandy, Mike, and John
You are the wind beneath my wings

Contents

Chronology

June 16, 1862	Alma Bridwell's birth
November 8, 1878	Alma Bridwell's conversion
December 21, 1887	Alma Bridwell marries Kent White
March 14, 1889	birth of Arthur Kent White
August 24, 1892	birth of Ray Bridwell White
March 6, 1893	Alma White's sanctification
July 7, 1896	first independent mission established (Denver)
December 29, 1901	founding of Pentecostal Union (Pillar of Fire)
March 16, 1902	ordination of Alma White
1908	church headquarters transferred from Denver to Zarephath, N.J.
August 11, 1909	Kent separates from Alma
1913	*Good Citizen* established (discontinued 1933)
September 1, 1918	Alma's consecration as bishop; church discipline adopted
1920	purchase of Westminster College (Denver)
1924	*Woman's Chains* established (discontinued 1970)
1927	purchase of KPOF radio station in Denver
1931	purchase of WAWZ radio station in Zarephath
1937	completion of Alma Temple in Denver
June 26, 1946	Alma White's death
1946	Arthur White assumes leadership of Pillar of Fire

1978   Arlene White Lawrence becomes president and
             general superintendent of Pillar of Fire

1984   Donald Wolfram becomes president and general
             superintendent of Pillar of Fire

Foreword

Alma White (1862–1946) was a fundamentalist feminist bishop. Today fundamentalists are hardly feminists, and feminists are rarely bishops. Yet Alma White was all three.

Alma White grew up in the holiness tradition of the Wesleyan movement in late nineteenth-century America. She was a shy and awkward young woman, but her successful pursuit of sanctification (achieved in 1893) eventually crushed the "man-fearing spirit" that limited her life and released in her great energies for ministry.

Professor Stanley has written a winsome biography of this unusual woman. Rejected by the Methodists because of her success as an evangelist, because of her preaching about holiness, and because of her gender, Alma White founded her own church, the Pillar of Fire. She could find no scriptural grounds for prohibiting women from preaching the Gospel or from leadership in the church. She acted on that conviction.

Alma White drew upon her Wesleyan/Holiness heritage to affirm women's rights in the church. This meant that while she was passionately biblical in her theology, she was never rigid about scriptural texts. She agreed with Calvinist fundamentalists who rejected modernism (evolutionary theory and higher biblical criticism), calling herself a fundamentalist. Yet at the same she refused the idea that Scripture had to be inerrant in order for the Bible to be valued as an authoritative source of doctrine, thus keeping herself apart from narrow Calvinist fundamentalism and leaving room for the experience of the Spirit.

Alma White was also a feminist, preaching that the Gospel of Jesus Christ liberated women from limitations linked to gender. Her life is a good example of the connection between feminism and sectarianism. Both movements challenge the status quo and religious authorities. The story of Alma White shows once again why there is a consistent feminist thrust to sectarian Christianity in the history of the church.

And finally, Alma White was a bishop, overseeing the ecclesiastical life of her church and using her pastoral and public power to continue the campaign for women's rights. Historians sometimes argue that the woman's rights movement died in the 1920s, only to be resurrected in the 1960s. Alma White is an exception to that pattern, sustaining a ministry devoted to feminist causes throughout the 1920s and 1930s. Her radical feminist journal *Woman's Chains* was devoted to promoting women's rights and the National Woman's Party, and encouraging women to vote.

Yet Alma White was a woman of her times who also became involved in things that make contemporary readers uneasy. Professor Stanley is honest in her research, pointing out Alma White's "unholy alliance" with the Ku Klux Klan. As a sectarian protestant church leader, White feared established religion and worried about the growing influx of Roman Catholic immigrants into twentieth-century American society. She was further disturbed by Roman Catholic opposition to women's suffrage. When these concerns were combined with her uncritical patriotism, she became convinced that the Klan was God's instrument for eliminating the "Catholic threat" to American values.

It is important to appreciate, however, the passion and enthusiasm of Alma White for causes that many of her contemporary Christians never supported. She was a product of her times, but she was also far ahead of her day—claiming her power as a woman to serve God and working unceasingly to promote equality for all women. As in the children's story about the little red hen that asks for help but repeatedly fails to receive the support she needs, the story of Alma White is the story of a woman who "did it herself." In the best of all worlds such women ought to have better support to keep them balanced, but the real world is rarely that generous. What Alma White did deserves our admiration. Professor Stanley has enhanced our knowledge about the Wesleyan/Holiness tradition, about the women's rights movement, and about a significant twentieth-century woman. We are in her debt.

BARBARA BROWN ZIKMUND
President, Hartford Seminary

Acknowledgments

My introduction to Alma White was a brief reference to her magazine *Woman's Chains* in an article by Donald Dayton and Lucille Sider Dayton.[1] I am indebted to the Daytons and to Nancy Hardesty for the groundwork they laid in researching women and feminism within the Wesleyan/Holiness movement.

This study could not have been undertaken without the support of Arlene White Lawrence, Alma White's granddaughter. She provided access to Alma's writings, both published and unpublished, which yielded knowledge not available elsewhere. Much of this book's biographical data comes from Alma's writings, including *The Story of My Life and the Pillar of Fire,* which chronicles her life through 1925, and her diaries, which furnished information from then until her death. The diaries, and other significant material, became available to me after I completed my dissertation on Alma White in 1987. I appreciated Bishop Lawrence's gracious hospitality during several visits to Zarephath, New Jersey. It is disappointing that the book was not completed before her death. Other Pillar of Fire members have also been helpful, particularly Bishop Robert Dallenbach, vice president and assistant superintendent of the Pillar of Fire, who granted permission to quote from Alma White's writings and use photographs. Alma Beth (Heidi) Dallenbach Walker, Alma White's great-granddaughter, helped select photographs. Cheryl and Keith Snyder and Jim Pearsall facilitated my research. Jim Pearsall's assistance was enhanced by our common interest in Pillar of Fire history.

Joyce Goodfriend, Jean Miller Schmidt, and the late Barbara Hargrove first encouraged and supervised my research at the University of Denver and the Iliff School of Theology.

Dean James Field of Western Evangelical Seminary granted me a sabbatical to complete the book. Patricia Rushford, writer in residence at Western Evangelical Seminary, read the manuscript and offered constructive suggestions. I am also grateful to my research assistants, particularly Chris Prescott, whose attention to details proved helpful in tracking down elusive facts.

As Carolyn Heilbrun has said, "I do not believe that new stories will find their way into texts if they do not begin in oral exchanges among women in groups hearing and talking to one another."[2] I thank those women (and men) in seminary and college classes, churches, and Women's Political Caucus meetings, and others around numerous dinner tables who have listened to my recitations of Alma's story. Their interest has inspired me to continue exploring Alma's life and telling her story.

This was a family project from start to finish. I thank my parents, Clayton and Sue Cunningham, for a Wesleyan/Holiness upbringing (in Kentucky) that helped me understand Alma White's religious faith. My mother also spent hours deciphering Alma's handwriting as she transcribed her diaries. My children have grown up with Alma during the twelve years I have been researching her life. Mike introduced me to the computer, patiently explaining its intricacies, and helped with proofreading. Mandy helped photocopy materials in libraries around the country. My husband John served as a sounding board, participating in hours of discussion, from my first visit to Alma Temple in 1981 to the day the manuscript was mailed to the editor. His enthusiasm and commitment have kept me going; he has always been there, providing encouragement and support.

Introduction

The links in the women's movement grew particularly weak between the 1920s and the 1960s. But even in the bleakest times and most barren places the light was kept alive by at least a few stalwart women who carried on the cause of feminism.
—MARY P. RYAN

Alma White (1862–1946) invalidates Mary Ryan's claim that the struggle for women's rights ended during the 1920s.[1] She was one of those stalwart women who proclaimed her commitment to feminism in an age when there were few feminist apologists. Feminism to Alma meant that "in every sphere of life, whether social, political, or religious, there must be equality between the sexes."[2] Described as "a Cromwell in skirts" and "almost terrifying in her intense earnestness,"[3] Alma militantly promoted feminism throughout her career, arguing that "a narrow mind may fail to grasp [women's equality], and it may take other sledge-hammer blows to release the public mind from the old traditions against equality of the sexes."[4] Heavyset and standing five feet eight inches tall, Alma's appearance accentuated her forceful demeanor. In an effort to demolish inequality she indeed wielded sledgehammer blows in the pulpit and through her writings.

Alma White exemplifies the "subversive potential" of religious belief.[5] Her life and publications demonstrate that Christianity can play a positive role in the liberation of women. Recognizing the liberating potential within Christianity, she zealously preached a feminist message, appropriating a biblical hermeneutic that corroborated her position.

But Alma was not naive. She acknowledged the role Christianity had played in thwarting women's autonomy. She rejected male domination of the institutional church by forming the Pentecostal Union (soon popularly known as the Pillar of Fire), through which she performed her ministry independently of patriarchal restrictions. She created an autonomous milieu that few women experience within the institutional church.

Alma's ministry and message reveal that feminism and Christianity can be compatible. She defined her religious calling in terms of

1

achieving equality for women and exhibited an astute awareness of the source of women's inequality: "Whenever woman has failed to scale the heights of human progress it has been because man forged her chains and kept her in subordination and thraldom."[6] Empowered by the Holy Spirit, Alma snapped the chains that fettered her and sought to free other women from religious, political, and social chains.

Alma actualized the feminist impulses inherent in Wesleyan/Holiness theology. Donald Dayton claims that "no other tradition in Christianity has been so feminist or so committed to the full ministry of women as the variety of traditions that in the nineteenth century took up the doctrine of 'Christian Perfection' or 'entire sanctification.'"[7] Her life confirms the thesis that the empowerment of the Holy Spirit that accompanies the experience of sanctification "compelled women to burst the cocoon of 'woman's sphere.'"[8] The doctrine of sanctification provided a social ethic that challenged the prevalent belief in woman's sphere, which maintained that a woman's place was in the home. Alma, along with other women in the Wesleyan/Holiness movement, relied on the power of the Holy Spirit to break through male-created barriers erected in an attempt to inhibit their activities outside the home.

Alma represents the hundreds of women ministers in the Wesleyan/Holiness movement, which at a time when most denominations denied women access to their pulpits claimed that God called both men and women to preach.[9] Women clergy served in the Salvation Army, the Church of God (Anderson, Indiana), and the Church of the Nazarene as well as in other, smaller Wesleyan/Holiness groups. For instance, Mary Lee Cagle founded eighteen congregations that merged with the Church of the Nazarene in 1908, making her "one of the co-founders" of that denomination.[10] Yet only a few groups outside the Wesleyan/Holiness movement ordained women at the turn of the century. Statistics for 1892 indicate that denominations that were not Wesleyan/Holiness reported less than seventy ordained women in the United States.[11] The Congregational church (now the United Church of Christ) listed only "a score or more" women clergy in 1920, compared to 350 women clergy in the Church of the Nazarene.[12] The most recent statistics show that women in five denominations in the Wesleyan/Holiness movement currently constitute 25 percent of the clergy in their denominations, whereas women comprise 7 percent of the clergy in thirty-nine other denominations that now ordain women.[13] The Wesleyan/Holiness movement has been at the forefront in affirming women's rights in the church.

Alma White established the Pillar of Fire to set "the example of equality for the sexes . . . by breaking the shackles that have held women in bondage for ages."[14] The media often observed her feminist emphasis: "One of the chief objects of Mrs. White's ministry," it was reported, "is the championing of woman's cause."[15] She described her church's guiding principles as "emancipation for women and ultra-fundamentalist doctrine."[16] Fundamentalist feminist? The phrase appears to be an oxymoron. Yet Alma White espoused a feminist agenda promoting women's rights in all areas of life and described herself as a fundamentalist.

When Alma declared, "We stand for fundamentalism,"[17] she aligned herself with opponents of modernism. Modernists promoted higher criticism of the Bible and evolution, which, to Alma and the fundamentalists, were creations of the devil. When fundamentalism is simply understood as "militant opposition to modernism,"[18] Alma qualifies as a fundamentalist. Most Wesleyan/Holiness leaders were "innocent bystanders"[19] who remained on the sidelines during the fundamentalist/modernist controversy of the late nineteenth and early twentieth centuries. Alma was an exception. She plunged into the midst of the fray to vigorously attack modernism.

An examination of Alma's theology, however, belies her claim that she and her church were guided by ultrafundamentalist doctrine. There were several key differences between Alma White's views and fundamentalism. Most fundamentalists were Calvinists, whereas Alma, whose Arminian theology reflected her Wesleyan roots, saw herself as a promoter of old-fashioned Methodism. Rather than introducing new doctrines, she stressed the New Testament ideals that initially had characterized Methodism. However, her switch from the postmillennialism of the Methodists to premillennialism mirrors the shift made by many holiness advocates in the late nineteenth century.[20] Alma distanced herself, though, from dispensationalism, which became a popular version of premillennialism among fundamentalists: "We are premillennialists and believe that Christ is coming soon. But we do not harp on Bible prophecy as do many of the modern fundamentalists."[21]

Another contrast between Alma and fundamentalists was the latter's doctrine of inerrancy,[22] the view that the Bible is without error in every detail. I have yet to find a reference to inerrancy in Alma's writings or sermons. Her doctrinal statement on the Bible affirmed that "the Scriptures are given by inspiration of God, and that they are 'the only sufficient rule of faith and practise.'"[23] Like other Wesleyan/Holiness preachers, she valued the Bible as an authoritative source of doctrine without claiming it is inerrant.

Other theological differences separated Alma from the fundamentalists. For the most part, fundamentalists valued a rational approach to Christianity, whereas Alma emphasized experience: "People may accept theories and doctrines and embrace creeds, but no one can have a personal knowledge of Christ until it comes to him through the revelation of the Holy Spirit. One must have an experience that goes infinitely deeper than a mere mental acceptance of Christ."[24] Further, most fundamentalists were separatists when it came to the world of politics. In contrast, Alma played an active role in seeking to transform society through the political process. She wrote letters to governors and representatives in Congress and even mailed telegrams to presidents, offering unsolicited advice on national and international affairs. She was an optimist regarding the possibility of political reform, whereas most fundamentalists were pessimists.

Alma was clearly at odds with a fundamentalism that was "inhospitable" to feminism.[25] Fundamentalists opposed the ordination of women, basing their position on a literal interpretation of 1 Corinthians 14:34–35 and 1 Timothy 2:11–12 (while ignoring other verses that support women's ministry). One would be hard pressed to find a fundamentalist, or anyone other than a member of the National Woman's Party, who shared Alma's unqualified support of the Equal Rights Amendment during the 1920s, 1930s, and 1940s.

Alma's claim that her theology was ultrafundamentalist does not accurately reflect her theological inclinations, then, because several critical doctrinal differences distinguished her theology from fundamentalism. Alma agreed wholeheartedly, however, with the fundamentalist critique of modernism. Fundamentalists' enemies were her enemies.

This book is a narrative biography, focusing on Alma's story as it relates to her spiritual development and her leadership of the Pillar of Fire. Chapter 1 covers the first thirty years of Alma's life, chronicling her childhood in Kentucky and her conversion, which was a crucial milepost among those who valued a revivalistic approach to Christianity. It also recounts her teaching career in Montana, her marriage to Kent White, and the birth of their two children.

Carolyn Heilbrun observed that "men tend to move on a fairly predictable path to achievement; women transform themselves only after an awakening."[26] Alma's awakening was her sanctification experience. Sanctification is a distinct second work of grace following conversion, the first work of grace. Empowered by the Holy Spirit as a result of her sanctification in 1893, Alma began working as an evangelist in Colorado and in surrounding states. Chapter 2 documents her early years of ministry and the founding of the Pentecostal Union in 1901.

Chapter 3 demonstrates how Alma's continuing pursuit of autonomy influenced her leadership style and her marriage. For several years, she worked closely with a compatible religious organization called the Burning Bush. Conflict over valuable real estate in New Jersey ended their cooperative ministry. Although Alma paid lip service to the prevailing view that the husband was the head of the home, her actions negated her words. Alma's quest for autonomy contributed to marital tension and, eventually, separation. Alma ruled her church with an iron hand, and she succeeded, in part, because of her autocratic leadership style. Had it been otherwise, it is doubtful she could have established a network of branches in the United States and London, overseen schools and printing facilities, published six magazines, authored more than thirty-five books, and purchased two radio stations.

Chapter 4 analyzes Alma's involvement in the Ku Klux Klan, her support of the National Woman Party's (NWP) feminist agenda, and her ministry in the remaining years of her life. Alma believed the Ku Klux Klan was a positive response to the problems the United States faced in the 1920s. She aligned herself with the KKK to attack perceived threats to conservative religion from Catholics and to protect the American way of life from the millions of immigrants landing on America's shores.

To achieve her feminist goals, Alma endorsed the National Woman's Party, the militant fringe of the woman's rights movement in the United States and the only self-defined feminist group in the 1920s. When the NWP introduced the Equal Rights Amendment in Congress in December 1923, Alma promptly exhibited her wholehearted support by publishing *Woman's Chains,* a periodical promoting the amendment and highlighting women's achievements in politics, business, and the church.

What first impressed me about Alma White was that she was a Wesleyan/Holiness woman who believed so fervently in women's rights that she established a magazine to promote her views. I was amazed by the radically feminist illustrations in *Woman's Chains.* Alma was a prophetic leader whose feminist views transcended the prejudices of her contemporaries.

I was shocked to learn that Alma White worked with the Ku Klux Klan. How could a woman with such a solid grasp of issues relating to justice for women be so blind to the unjust agenda of the KKK? This question still haunts me. But like many others of her generation, she equated a misguided patriotism with religion—a temptation many Christians face today. Alma did not rise above the xenophobia prevalent in the 1920s. Several scholars have documented her involvement in the Ku Klux Klan, but no studies of feminism include Alma's support of the Equal Rights Amendment.[27] As leader of the only denomination to endorse the Equal Rights Amendment at its inception, Alma deserves to be listed among those who kept feminism alive between the 1920s and the 1960s.

1
Prelude to Ministry

CHILDHOOD

My feelings often they would hurt,
And never did they care
How hard that life was made for me,
Or what I had to bear.
— ALMA WHITE, *Musings of the Past*

Mollie Alma, as she was known until midlife, was born on June 16, 1862, to William and Mary Ann Bridwell in Lewis County, Kentucky.[1] Six other daughters and four sons made up the Bridwell family.

Alma endured an unhappy childhood. Following the Civil War, the economic situation in Kentucky was grim. Alma's parents had hoped for a son to compensate for the shortage of male workers due to the war. Whether a boy or a girl, however, each Bridwell child, was expected "to do his or her part in helping to make a living." The fact that her parents frequently voiced their displeasure that Alma was a girl pained her: "It was sometimes difficult to dispel the gloom that forced itself into the silent chambers of my heart."[2]

Alma recalled a dreary childhood of monotonous chores, including pulling weeds in the vegetable patches, feeding the chickens, gathering wood, and carrying drinking water to the house. Indoor responsibilities included watching younger siblings. When she grew older, she assisted her father in his tannery by placing the animal hides in vats between layers of bark, which she then helped grind. The economic effects of the Civil War plagued the family into the 1870s. Because of high prices, there was "a constant struggle, with so large a family, to make ends meet."[3] There was some respite from Alma's dreary existence. Occasionally she received permission to walk along the Kinniconick River near her home and enjoy the beautiful scenery. She also grew flowers, touch-me-nots being her favorite, in designated areas of the garden.

Alma provided little information on her physical appearance as a child, other than brief references to her size and her hair. She disclosed:

7

"I was overgrown for my age, and looked upon by everyone as being the odd and less attractive one of the family." Her only positive feature was her hair: "Until I was eleven or twelve my hair hung down my back in curls."[4] Others often compared Alma unfavorably with her younger sister, Theresa West.

The Bridwell home nestled in the hillside above the banks of the Kinniconick. William Moncure Bridwell, Alma's father, had moved to Kentucky from Virginia, the original home of many Kentuckians. He had married Mary Ann Harrison, a native of Lewis County, and purchased a tannery on the river in Lewis County shortly before the war. The river afforded water, and the oaks towering over the Bridwell home provided the bark required to complete the tanning process.

Alma's family moved to Vanceburg, the county seat, in the fall of 1869, so her older brother and sisters could attend school. Mr. Bridwell secured a job in a steam tannery, and Mrs. Bridwell sewed men's suits in order to support the family. At the close of the school year, the family moved back to their home on the river. They had moved their house up the hill so it would be less damp and farther from the tannery vats, which were hazardous for curious small children. Alma had already experienced one rescue from the awful mixture of bark pieces and animal hides and had once pulled her two-year-old brother, Charles, from the vats. Charles, ten years younger than Alma, was her favorite sibling.

As a child and a young adult, Alma suffered from low self-esteem. One highlight of her girlhood was a visit from her uncle, Martin Bridwell, a police officer from Knoxville, Tennessee. Alma overheard Uncle Martin say, "If she [Alma] gets started right she will make her mark in the world and succeed as no other child you have."[5] Her uncle's indirect encouragement meant a great deal to the ten-year-old.

CONVERSION

After seven years as a penitent
I had at last come to the end of the struggle
and received the uncontainable blessing.

—ALMA WHITE, *Story of My Life*

There was no church within five miles of Alma's home, so the Bible, a hymnal, and John Bunyan's *Pilgrim's Progress* served as primary sources for her religious education. Her parents were known for their religious orthodoxy. Alma's mother was Methodist, and her father had been raised a Baptist and, at one time, had been licensed as an exhorter, someone who encouraged people to respond to a pastor's sermon by committing themselves to Christ. Alma listened with rapt attention as her father discussed and debated religious issues with relatives and neighbors. She learned about the Christian church as her father argued with her uncle, Dick Thomas, who had embraced the teaching of Alexander Campbell, the church's founder. Enunciating Campbell's views, which attracted many followers in Kentucky, Uncle Dick contended that baptism was essential for the forgiveness of sins and that immersion was the only requirement for becoming a Christian. Alma's father argued that a personal experience of conversion, or new birth resulting in a change of heart, was necessary. Conversion occurred instantaneously when one's sins were forgiven and one committed one's life to Christ. Due to his Baptist background, Bridwell believed in baptism by immersion, but later, as a result of controversies with Dick Thomas and other followers of Alexander Campbell, he adopted the position that baptism be conferred by sprinkling or pouring water on the candidate. He felt that immersion could contribute to the mistaken belief that one's sins are actually washed away. In 1874 Bridwell became affiliated with the Methodist Episcopal church, which performed the sacrament of baptism by sprinkling or pouring.

During the heated religious discussions with Uncle Dick, other family members graphically described hell as a literal place reserved for sinners after death. The conversations aroused a fear in Alma's heart that she was destined for hell. Alma, who was nine at the time, wished to be converted in order to avoid hell, yet no one, according to Alma, talked to her about the state of her soul.

Alma joined the Methodist Episcopal church when she was twelve years old. Anticipating the Civil War, the church had separated into northern and southern factions in 1844. A convention held in Louisville in May 1845 created the Methodist Episcopal Church, South. At the end of the war, the northern branch claimed three thousand members in Kentucky, whereas more than forty-five thousand belonged to the southern branch.[6] Rev. S. G. Pollard, who was a pastor with the Methodist Episcopal church, the name retained by the northern branch, traveled from Vanceburg, Kentucky, to conduct revival meetings five miles from Alma's home in 1874. During the revival services, Alma, along with her father and several other family members, began the six-month probation period that was required before becoming full members of the Methodist Episcopal church. Alma had yet to experience conversion.

Church membership did not satisfy Alma's religious longing. She continued to seek conversion, but sporadic church attendance and minimal contact with ministers meant that she never had the chance to fulfill her desire. Alma had decided that "it would be impossible to get converted outside a revival meeting,"[7] yet Rev. Pollard's revival had not resulted in her conversion. She began to despair: "Night after night, after every other member of the family had retired, I stood at the window in the dining room praying and looking at the stars, until after twelve o'clock; and would sometimes remain there until I heard the clock strike two or three."[8]

Alma's preoccupation with conversion reflected a concern present among most Protestants of the nineteenth century. Members of Reformed groups, Congregationalists, Presbyterians, and Baptists, as well as Methodists, sought the experience. Their search, like Alma's, followed a predictable pattern, which included an awareness of personal sin and the possibility of going to hell.[9]

Two years later, in the fall of 1876, Rev. J. S. Sims became pastor of the Methodist Episcopal Church, South, congregation in Vanceburg.[10] He preached at the local schoolhouse in Alma's neighborhood once a month on Thursday nights. The pastor soon formed a local class meeting, and the Bridwells transferred their church membership from the northern branch of Methodism to this fledgling group. Although Kentucky was a border state, many of its citizens, including the Bridwells, strongly identified with the South. Alma continued to attend the services, but conversion remained beyond her grasp. During this time, she and several of her siblings attended a religious meeting several miles away at Northcutt chapel. Again, Alma listened intently, but no invitation was given at the end of the sermon to come forward and become a Christian. Had someone invited her to go to the altar and pray, Alma believed she would have experienced conversion: "A little spiritual instruction at this time would have helped me into the kingdom, but no one offered me such assistance, and I knew of nothing else to do but to pray and wait for another preacher to come." Alma continued to seek conversion: "For weeks and months I lived in the shadows of Sinai, fearing that God's lightning would strike me any moment and seal my doom for time and eternity. Oh, how miserable I was!"[11]

It wasn't until she was sixteen that Alma became a Christian during a revival conducted by William B. Godbey, the new pastor in Vanceburg who replaced Rev. Sims in 1878. Alma attended the first service Godbey conducted in her neighborhood and observed that he preached with his eyes closed because they were sensitive to light. He dressed in plain clothes and tied a white handkerchief around his neck. Soon after his arrival, Rev. Godbey announced that he would conduct a pro- tracted meeting in Alma's neighborhood. These revival services were a legacy of the camp meetings, the most famous of which took place in nearby Cane Ridge, Kentucky, in August 1801. By the time Alma arrived on the momentous evening of November 8, 1878, Holly School was full of the curious who had come to see Godbey. A third- generation Methodist preacher, born and educated in Kentucky, he had pastored for twenty-five years before assuming the pulpit at Vance- burg.

Somewhat of an eccentric, Godbey never used a short word when a four- or five-syllable alternative would suffice. An eulogist mentioned Godbey's love of words: "His vocabulary was extensive. He revelled in words. He studied words, he dug up words, he coined words, he used words that few other persons ever heard of!" While admitting his "penchant for unusual words" and "his odd appearance," the author of Godbey's obituary also declared that his name would "loom large in that part of [church history] dealing with the revival which came to Methodism during the latter part of the last century."[12]

Due to the crowd, Alma had to sit in front of the room on the mourners' bench, which was generally empty until the close of the ser- vice when non-Christians came forward to mourn their sins and pray for forgiveness. Alma was so close to the preacher that at one point during the sermon he accidently hit her on the head while gesturing. The text for the evening was Romans 6:23 ("For the wages of sin is death, but the free gift of God is eternal life in Jesus Christ our Lord"). The sermon dealt specifically with how one became a Christian. Alma had been waiting for a sermon like this. Rev. Godbey's descriptions of hell, referred to as "the most awful piece of sacred oratory . . . ever heard,"[13] caused some of the congregation to become so upset that they had to leave the room and throw up. Alma responded to the altar call at the conclusion of the sermon and knelt to pray. Rev. Godbey knelt at her side and counseled her. Alma prayed, confessing her sins and accepting Jesus' forgiveness. As a result of her repentance and faith in Jesus, she experienced conversion, and her search for salvation came to an end. She rejoiced in her new identity as a Christian: "After seven years a penitent I had at last come to the end of the battle. The burden of sin had rolled away . . . It was as if I had been lifted out of hell into heaven."[14] Alma's fear of hell vanished; she knew heaven was her ultimate home. Naturally, Alma's evaluation of the minister whose preaching led her to the experience of salvation was high: "There was no other preacher like W. B. Godbey." From this moment, her admiration of Godbey never faltered. She later wrote in her autobiography, "The years that have intervened have confirmed me in this belief."[15]

Soon after her conversion, Alma decided she would become a preacher—a highly unusual aspiration for a young woman. A woman's right to preach was not recognized officially by the Methodist Episcopal Church, South, or by most other Protestant churches. As Alma pondered her future, perhaps she read the article "May Women Preach?" printed in her denominational magazine. Written in 1881, the author answered the question posed in the title with an emphatic no.[16] Probably dissuaded by the negative attitude toward women ministers reflected in this article, Alma soon accommodated her career goal to the stereotypical limitations imposed on the women of her day: "I wanted to tell what [God] had done for me, and made up my mind to preach the Gospel if I had to go to a foreign land as a missionary in order to do it."[17] She was among the many women during the late nineteenth century who initially set aside their calling to preach and considered the alternative of working in the foreign mission field. By 1880, 57 percent of the active missionaries from the United States were women.[18] The Methodist Episcopal Church, South, founded the Woman's Missionary Society in 1878, the year of Alma's conversion. Local societies raised money and sent Dora and Lochie Rankin to China during the society's first year of operation.[19] The promotion of missions by women in her denomination may have influenced Alma's career decision.

EDUCATION AND TEACHING OUT WEST

I knew that I must make preparations to preach the Gospel, either in the homeland or in a foreign field and determined to seek for an open door, and to enter it at the earliest possible opportunity. It occurred to me that I could find this door as a school teacher,—that I could begin with my pupils and their parents,—and this conviction deepened.

—ALMA WHITE, *Story of My Life*

Soon after her conversion, Alma talked to Rev. Godbey about becoming a preacher. He attempted to steer her away from this profession by advising her to become a minister's wife where, he contended, she would have "a wide field for Christian work."[20] Being a minister's wife was "one of the most coveted careers available to American women" in the nineteenth century.[21] It provided a position of religious influence otherwise unaccessible to most women. Disregarding Godbey's advice to marry a pastor, at least for the time being, Alma chose to become a missionary. Perhaps inspired by Lochie Rankin, who taught in China for forty-nine years, Alma decided to pursue teacher training in preparation to fulfill her religious calling.

Home duties kept Alma from attending school on a regular basis until she was eleven. Prior to this time, her mother taught Alma to read at home, using Webster's *Elementary Spelling Book*. Not withstanding her meager educational background and her family's belief that her sisters were smarter, Alma placed first in a spelling contest in 1874 at the close of her first year in school and won a prized leather, gilt-edged Bible with a clasp. One of the competitors in the contest was her sister Nora.

In 1879, at the conclusion of her schooling at the local level, Alma began attending the Vanceburg Female Seminary. Because Vanceburg was nine miles from home, Alma and two of her sisters boarded with a local family. The principal of the school observed Alma's shyness and advised her father that it might affect her studies. The principal's prediction proved wrong. Alma passed the teacher certification test and received a second-class, first-grade teacher certificate and accepted a short-term teaching assignment in a nearby district.

In the spring of 1880, the family moved seventy miles to Millersburg, Kentucky, so Alma and other members of the family could continue their education. Alma enrolled at the Millersburg Female College, a school established by Methodists in 1852. Although she had not yet graduated, her second certification test, in the summer of 1881, resulted in a first-class teaching certificate. With her certificate in hand, Alma secured a teaching position in the local school district.

Despite her ease in obtaining a job, all was not well in Alma's life. She reflected on deteriorating family relationships:

> I seemed to be in the way at home, and there was no longer peaceful adjustment of differences that came up between me and other members of the family. . . . Mother, who usually had given me some consideration in her efforts to keep peace, changed in her attitude toward me and made decisions that I knew to be unjust and that I felt hurt her conscience.[22]

Alma provided only a few examples of unjust treatment, primarily instances in which her parents seemed to favor her sisters. One such instance occurred when she was over eighteen: her mother ordered her to wear a hat that her sister Lida had discarded, and when Alma refused, her mother hit her across the shoulders with a tree limb.[23] Alma's assessment of her home life maintained its negative tone: "Life at home had been one of hardship and disappointment. Occasionally, I had gathered roses along the pathway but often walked on beds of thorns."[24] Without collaborative evidence, it is impossible to determine the extent of Alma's mistreatment. Was her evaluation accurate or was it colored by her lack of self-esteem or her self-consciousness due to her size? Whatever the case, Alma contemplated leaving home to escape what seemed to her a hostile environment.

Eliza Mason, Alma's aunt, offered Alma the opportunity. Aunt Eliza had visited Kentucky in the summer of 1881 and offered to take Lida or Nora, her favorite nieces, to live with her and her husband, D. B. Mason, in Montana Territory. When Alma's sisters declined the invitation, Aunt Eliza reluctantly agreed to allow Alma to come the following spring.

Alma recorded her parents' reaction to her upcoming departure:

> Mother, perhaps, could not have felt worse if she had been following my remains to the tomb. Father lost his appetite, and for three days before my departure pushed back from unfinished meals. His eyes were red with weeping; and when I left him at the depot he was so overcome he could scarcely speak.[25]

This statement, revealing her parents' emotional response to her departure, contrasts with Alma's bleak picture of her relationship with them. Evidently, by her own account here, her parents cared for her more than she generally admitted. Her low self-esteem clouded her judgment in assessing others' concern and love for her.

Alma, now nineteen years old, departed for Montana by train on March 20, 1882, at the conclusion of her winter term of teaching. Prior to this time, her only trip outside Kentucky had been one brief visit across the Ohio River to Aberdeen, Ohio. Despite delays due to flooding, fears of being abducted by Mormon polygamists in Utah, and one frightening interval when she was the only woman in a passenger car full of cowboys, Alma arrived safely at her destination, Bannack. A small town nestled in the Rocky Mountains, Bannack was located in southwest Montana, about twenty miles from Dillon. Bannack had been the center of early gold mining activities in Montana Territory.

Other single women teachers had preceded Alma to the territory, seeking their fortunes through marriage to wealthy miners or cattle barons. Heeding Rev. Godbey's admonition to marry a preacher, Alma insisted that she was not interested in marrying for money: "I was not on the market to be picked up by the wealthy bachelors or widowers who had bank accounts, gold mines, and cattle ranches. . . . No person but a preacher of the Gospel had any chance of winning my favor."[26] Alma did not scrutinize the eligible bachelors but commenced teaching, earning a salary of sixty dollars a month, almost double her Kentucky wages.

Two years later, during the spring of 1884, Alma traveled home to Kentucky, where she resumed her schooling for a year at Millersburg Female College. Alma returned to Montana a year later but discovered that no teaching positions were available.

At the annual conference of the Methodist Episcopal church held in Dillon in July 1885, Alma spoke to the ministers, sharing the story of her conversion. Apparently, this was the first time she had addressed clergy at an annual conference. Alma met Rev. Thomas C. Iliff, the superintendent of the Methodist mission work in Utah, at the conference. He offered her a teaching position in Salt Lake City, which she gratefully accepted.

The year Alma taught in Utah was the closest she came to serving as a missionary, because the Woman's Home Missionary Society of her denomination underwrote the expenses of her school. However, her working relationship with this agency disillusioned her:

> Life in the Mormon capital was not a bed of roses for me. There were many thorns along my pathway in this city of the so-called prophets and saints. But my foes were not the followers of Joseph Smith or Brigham Young; they were in my own church fold, and were most uncharitable and bitter.[27]

The local pastor antagonized Alma by making sarcastic comments about the South in his sermons. Alma also discovered she was receiving lower wages and paying more for room and board than other teachers in the school. At the end of the school year, Alma suffered a physical collapse that she attributed to the strain caused by the problems she had encountered. Alma summed up the year in one terse statement: "Methodism in Salt Lake City had keenly disappointed me."[28]

Rev. Iliff offered Alma a position in any of the other Methodist schools under his supervision in Utah, but she refused. Seriously doubting that she could fulfill her calling to ministry within Methodism,

Alma returned to Montana and secured a teaching position at Lima,[29] a railroad town approximately forty miles south of Dillon.

COURTSHIP AND EARLY MARRIAGE

*I had never seen or heard of {Kent White} but it had come to me
when I met him at the door that he was to be my husband.
So deeply was I impressed with this thought I stayed up
nearly all night to pray.*

—ALMA WHITE, *Looking Back from Beulah*

Alma first met Kent White, her future husband, on March 3, 1883, while she was still living with her aunt and uncle in Bannack.[30] He had traveled from Fish Creek, Montana, to fill a three-day appointment in the local Methodist Episcopal church. Kent, born in Beverly, West Virginia, on August 16, 1860, had headed West in 1880, stopping in Utah several months before moving on to Idaho to work at Fort Hall Indian Reservation as an issue clerk and butcher. Two years later, he moved to Fish Creek, Montana, and began working on F. A. Riggin's ranch. Riggin, superintendent of the Montana Methodist Episcopal Mission, licensed Kent as a local preacher in September 1882.[31] Kent had come to Bannack at the request of Rev. William Van Orsdale.

Preachers generally stayed in Aunt Eliza's home when they visited Bannack. Alma was the first person to greet Kent when he came to the door. She and Kent found several opportunities for conversation, and she sensed immediately that Kent would play an important role in her future. Although the possibility of their meeting again "seemed vague and uncertain," Alma was "willing to await God's time for developments."[32] During his short stay, the two formed a friendship that continued by correspondence after Kent left.

Less than six months after their initial meeting, Alma traveled to Butte, Montana, to visit two uncles. Kent met her at the train station. Alma had timed the trip to coincide with a Methodist conference Kent would be attending at Butte. There he informed Alma that he was planning to enroll at the University of Denver to study for the ministry. Affiliated with the Methodist Episcopal church, the school offered a liberal arts program and seminary training for Methodist clergy.[33] Later, Kent visited Alma on his way to Denver and attempted to convince her to join him at school. Alma declined because she had already accepted a teaching position for the winter at a location three and a half miles from Dillon. The two exchanged letters more frequently after

Kent moved to Denver, but neither mentioned the future. Alma was adept at reading between the lines: "Too well I knew what was on his mind, though not a word had been said or a suggestion made."[34]

Alma and Kent became engaged in November 1886, while she was teaching in Lima. Kent proposed via letter: "Sister Bridwell, I give you the assurance that I love you. . . . Today the divine will seems to say take her hand and lead her gently through the lights and shades of life until your mission is done and your reward cometh."[35] Kent confessed that at times he had doubted Alma's love and that he had attempted to suppress his love for her. Confident now of her love, he asked for her hand in marriage and suggested that they marry within a year. Alma answered Kent's letter promptly, agreeing to marry him and follow him wherever he was called to minister.[36] Kent rejoiced in his journal: "I believe firmly and truly that God had guided me and given me Miss Mollie Alma Bridwell to walk in life's lights and shades, to cheer and comfort me as I toil for my Master. Glory to God for His love and goodness! Amen, and amen!"[37]

Subsequent letters reveal the typical concerns of an engaged couple. Alma confessed that she once believed she was in love while she still lived in Kentucky but that the young man was attracted to one of her sisters. She assured Kent: "I thought I loved him then, but I knew after I saw you I did not—no comparison whatever." Alma also worried about pleasing her future mother-in-law. (Subsequent encounters with Kent's mother proved that her concern was well grounded.) Kent asked if Alma wanted an engagement ring. She left the decision up to him—and then regretted that he did not buy her one. The separation became unbearable for Kent, who wrote Alma in April: "I believe more and more the sooner we are together as husband and wife the better."[38] Alma completed the school year in Lima before moving to Denver in September 1887. During the summer, Kent had united with the Colorado Methodist Episcopal Conference and accepted an appointment as assistant pastor at Lupton, Colorado, while he continued his studies at the University of Denver. Alma taught part time in the grammar school associated with the university to earn money for classes in vocal and instrumental music and English literature at the university. Kent sold books to pay his expenses.

They married in the Asbury Methodist Episcopal Church in Denver on December 21, 1887, culminating a four-year courtship by correspondence. The twenty-five-year-old bride wore a traditional white gown with a train, even though her preference was a practical tailor-made outfit. Alma complied with Kent's desire for the gown, but she was "conscience-smitten" because of the added cost of the dress. They pursued their studies at the University of Denver and at a private college of elocution. Alma transferred her membership to Trinity Methodist Church in Denver, where she joined the choir.

Kent and Alma initially set up housekeeping in rented rooms, taking their meals in local restaurants. During the summer of 1888, they lived in Bishop Henry W. Warren's house while his family vacationed at the Pacific coast. Alma spoke of being "very ill" that summer, describing her sickness as being due to a weak heart, weak lungs, and poor circulation. She was also pregnant, which undoubtedly compounded her health problems.[39] At one point, she faulted Kent for his insensitivity to her condition. She had asked him for a piece of ice from a passing truck to quench her thirst, and Kent had run after the truck. He was gone for hours. In the meantime, Alma assumed her husband had encountered some terrible misfortune: "No words of tongue or pen can depict what I suffered in mind and body during those seven hours. Had some accident happened and disabled him? . . . I wept until my eyes were swollen."[40] In pursuit of the ice, Kent had remembered another commitment and promptly forgot about Alma's request. Within six months after her marriage, Alma was disillusioned: "I had taken a companion for better or worse, and my only hope was to overlook his imperfections."[41]

The relationship between Alma and Kent deteriorated rapidly when Kent's mother traveled from West Virginia in November 1888 for an extended visit. By this time, the couple had rented a house on Champa Street in Denver. Mary White took an immediate dislike to her daughter-in-law and, according to Alma, did everything in her power to antagonize her and create disharmony between the newlyweds. Mrs. White made Alma miserable by comparing her unfavorably to her own daughter, Lizzie. Rather than defending his wife, Kent sided with his mother, further fueling Alma's anguish. Alma remembered that they "held [Lizzie] up to me as a model young woman, intending this as a rebuke for me for what they considered my many failures." Among other things, Kent and his mother discussed the fact that Alma was "overgrown" and had "married above her station."[42] It seemed to Alma that Kent focused constantly on her faults and inadequacies. During this period, Alma suffered physical ailments that left her bedridden for four months. Her mother-in-law's presence undoubtedly contributed to Alma's suffering, and Kent's apparent lack of sympathy multiplied her agony.

Matters failed to improve with the birth of Arthur Kent White on March 14, 1889. Shortly after Arthur's birth, Alma contracted a painful breast infection. Neither Kent nor his mother acknowledged the seriousness of her illness, disregarding Dr. Wilson's instructions to contact him if her condition worsened. Alma endured excruciating pain before Mrs. White finally called in a nurse who was able to relieve her discomfort. When the doctor arrived, he upbraided both Kent and his mother for ignoring his orders and allowing Alma to suffer needlessly.

Mrs. White left for West Virginia on May 30, 1889, and Alma expressed relief at her departure: "I relaxed in both mind and body." But she wondered if the discord Mrs. White had fostered in her marriage could ever be overcome. Things appeared hopeful when Kent asked for her forgiveness, but Alma reported that Kent's repentance was not enough to "mend a broken heart and constitution, and build up in a few months what had been so ruthlessly torn down."[43]

Alma remained in poor health after Arthur's birth, contracting dropsy and enlargement of organs. She consulted a specialist in women's diseases but discontinued treatment when he made "improper advances." Alma offered her own diagnosis: "I knew that my condition was beyond medical skill, and that from a human standpoint I should never be any better." She spoke of herself as an "invalid wife"[44] who was unable to do her housework and take care of her baby.

Kent, meanwhile, progressed toward full ordination in the Methodist Episcopal church. At the Colorado annual conference in 1889, he was ordained a deacon and assigned churches in Lamar and Las Animas, Colorado. The previous year he had commuted one hundred miles by train on weekends to student appointments in churches at Hugo and Kit Carson, Colorado. He also had organized a class and Sunday school at Cheyenne Wells. After the annual conference, the family moved to Lamar, where they lived for the next two years. While at Lamar, Kent added sixty-five people to the church's membership and retired a $225 debt on the church building.[45] Kent was ordained an elder in 1891 and transferred to Morrison, Colorado, where he served another two years. The move to Morrison, in the foothills of the Rocky Mountains, was prompted by the hope that the mountain air would contribute to an improvement in Alma's health.

Kent's and Alma's second son, Ray Bridwell, was born in Morrison on August 24, 1892. Despite Alma's fears that her pregnancy was life threatening, she survived childbirth. Ray and Arthur were both sick as babies,[46] the former nearly dying from pneumonia during his first Christmas. Alma believed God allowed Ray to live after she promised to preach, regardless of the opposition she faced.

*"The Old Kentucky Home"—
Alma's home before it was
moved to Zarephath, N.J.*

*Alma, the school teacher,
c. 1881*

Alma's engagement picture, 1886

Kent holds Arthur while Alma holds Ray, 1892

Kent begins full-time evangelistic work in 1895

Alma fulfills her calling to preach as an evangelist, late 1890s

William B. Godbey, Alma's mentor, is the featured speaker at the camp meeting sponsored by the Colorado Holiness Association, 1896

Alma attends the General Holiness Assembly in Chicago, 1901

The White family poses shortly before their separation, c. 1909

Alma purchases her first car in 1913

WOMAN'S CHAINS

Vol. 1. No. 1.   Zarephath, N. J.,   January-February,   1924.   Price 10 Cents.

Cover of the first issue of Woman's Chains, *January-February 1924*

Alma and her granddaughter Arlene White (Lawrence), who later served as president and general superintendent of the Pillar of Fire (1978–1984), c. 1920

Woman's Chains, *May-June 1924*

Woman's Chains, *September-October 1925*

WE MUST HAVE EQUALITY IN THE HOME AND IN THE NATION

Woman's Chains, *January-February 1925*

Woman's Chains,
January-February 1924

Woman's Chains,
March-April 1927

WHAT YEAR?

Aerial view of Zarephath, N.J., 1924

Arthur and Ray serve as Alma's primary assistants, c. 1925

Alma broadcasts over Pillar of Fire radio station KPOF, 1928

ALMA TEMPLE, DENVER, COLORADO

13th AVENUE AND SHERMAN STREET

Church of the Pillar of Fire

Dedicated October 31, 1937

Although construction began in 1923, completion was delayed, primarily due to the depression

Alma enters her last years as leader of the Pillar of Fire, c. 1936

Alma begins painting in her seventies, c. 1940

2
Initiation of Ministry

SANCTIFICATION

*My soul was reaching out for something that would take me
to higher heights than I had ever gone in the Christian experience.*
—ALMA WHITE, *Story of My Life*

Alma knew there would have to be a drastic change in her personality before she would be able to preach and fulfill the promise she had made to God at Ray's sick bed. Because of her natural shyness, earlier efforts to testify had resulted in failure. She had looked for opportunities to speak during a revival meeting at Lamar the winter of 1890, but when the chance came, she was overcome with a "man-fearing spirit" that prevented her from speaking.[1] Other Wesleyan/Holiness women testified that sanctification crushed the man-fearing spirit that initially had inhibited their ministries.[2] Hoping that sanctification might help her overcome her shyness, Alma intensified her quest for this experience.

Alma had begun her pursuit of sanctification prior to 1883. This was one of the topics she and Kent had discussed during their first meeting in Bannack, Montana. *Perfection* and *holiness* are synonyms for *sanctification,* a second distinct work of grace, with *conversion* or *justification* being understood as the first work of grace. John Wesley, the founder of Methodism, pronounced his understanding of the doctrine in *A Plain Account of Christian Perfection.* He explained that a person attains Christian perfection

> when, after having been fully convinced of inbred sin by a far deeper and clearer conviction than that which he experienced before justification, and after having experienced a gradual mortification of it, he experiences a total death to sin and an entire renewal in the love and image of God, so as to rejoice evermore, to pray without ceasing, and in everything to give thanks.[3]

Wesley believed that the witness of the Holy Spirit established that a person possessed Christian perfection or sanctification: "None, therefore, ought to believe that the work is done, till there is added the testimony of the Spirit, witnessing his entire sanctification as clearly as his justification."[4]

Wesley's evangelists brought the doctrine of sanctification to the American colonies. Francis Asbury, whose ministry commenced in 1771, served as bishop of the Methodist Episcopal church from its founding in 1784 until his death in 1816. Asbury's diary entry for March 1, 1803, indicates that he sought to include a discussion of sanctification in every sermon.[5] As the years passed, however, the doctrine languished.

As a lay evangelist and author, Phoebe Palmer played a leading role in rekindling interest in sanctification during her remarkable ministry extending from 1839 to her death in 1874.[6] Influenced by the revivalistic atmosphere prevalent in the United States at the time, her view of sanctification differed somewhat from John Wesley's, even though she was Methodist. The prominent evangelist Charles Finney, Palmer's contemporary, had popularized the active dimension of conversion in his revival preaching.[7] Reflecting the emphasis on the active role of the individual, Palmer stressed that the experience of holiness, like conversion, could be had for the asking.[8] She began her popular book *The Way of Holiness* with a discussion of a "shorter way" to holiness: "I am sure that this long waiting and struggling with the powers of darkness is not necessary."[9] Palmer believed that holiness should be claimed immediately rather than after a prolonged quest. One did not need to wait until he or she received the witness of the Holy Spirit.[10] She contended that because God had promised sanctification, one should believe God's word. To do otherwise was to doubt God. The seeker must lay one's all on the altar, which is Christ, who then sanctifies the gift. Palmer testified: "I had *obtained* this blessing [of holiness], by *laying all upon the altar.*"[11]

By 1867, the fiftieth American printing of Palmer's *The Way of Holiness* appeared. Her books, the Tuesday Meeting for the Promotion of Holiness held in her home, and her extensive preaching of holiness throughout the United States introduced thousands to the doctrine. Consequently, the message of sanctification, as interpreted by Palmer, had permeated the Methodist Episcopal church by the mid-nineteenth century.[12]

Kent had experienced sanctification in West Virginia in 1876, a year after his conversion.[13] During his initial conversation with Alma, he mentioned a book written by J. A. Wood (probably *Perfect Love*) that explained the doctrine. Alma was "deeply interested,"[14] and although she had sought the experience, she confessed that she was not sanctified:

> I had heard sanctification preached, but had never clearly understood it as an experience obtainable in this life for any person who will meet conditions. I supposed it was for the high officiary of the church, and that laymen in the humble walks of life need not expect to get it.[15]

Initially Alma had assumed that achieving conversion signified the pinnacle of the Christian life. Now she realized that a higher level of Christian living was possible for all Christians. She had written Kent during their courtship in November 1883: "We have testimonials of numbers who testify to a perfect salvation—resting securely and peacefully in Jesus. Is it not for me? Something seems to say that it is if you will claim it."[16] For some reason, Alma was unable to answer her question in the affirmative.

While Alma was in Kentucky from the spring 1884 to the following spring, Kent had written, encouraging her to continue seeking sanctification. On her return trip to Montana, Alma stopped in Denver to see Kent. During the layover, Kent prayed with Alma that she would be sanctified but her efforts were unsuccessful. Shortly after her marriage, Rev. Godbey influenced Alma's life again through his book *Victory.*[17] Alma read this book on sanctification and listened to sermons on the topic, but she still did not personally experience sanctification.

Following Ray's illness, Alma was anxious to carry out her promise to preach but was unable to do so because of shyness. Her pursuit of sanctification became an obsession: "There was but little else on my mind."[18] In spite of her endeavors, sanctification remained beyond her grasp. From her reading, Alma understood that consecration, or total commitment to God, was a prerequisite for sanctification. She consecrated her life on the altar of Christ on March 6, 1893, but sanctification did not follow. Alma learned in a discussion with Finnis Yoakum of Denver that after fully consecrating her life, she simply should claim sanctification by faith.

Alma decided to fast and pray until sanctification was hers. After two days passed, Kent encouraged Alma with the words "the everlasting arms are about you." Alma meditated on the love of Christ and envisioned Christ dying for her on the cross. Alma reported that she attained the second work of grace "in the twinkling of an eye," when she accepted it by faith on March 18, 1893. No outburst of feeling accompanied the moment: "When the blessing of sanctification came there was no great outpouring of the Spirit, but simply a deep soul rest and the consciousness that my heart was pure."[19]

Alma's experience of sanctification paralleled the teaching of Phoebe Palmer, who explained how a person obtains sanctification: "There are but two steps to the blessing; ENTIRE CONSECRATION is the first; FAITH is the second."[20] Palmer taught that once these two steps were taken, sanctification occurred instantaneously.[21] Alma's understanding of the doctrine and Finnis Yoakum's advice reflect an awareness and appropriation of Palmer's theology.

Alma believed that sanctification cleansed her heart of inherited sin or depravity, and she reported "a deep realization of purity in the depths of my inmost soul such as I had never known before."[22] Alma contended, along with other holiness adherents, including John Wesley, that this purity resulted from the eradication of the sinful nature that every human possesses. They maintained that conversion involved the forgiveness of actual sins whereas sanctification removed "inbred defilement."[23]

EARLY PREACHING

I was sanctified March 18, 1893 . . . From that time forward my whole life was changed.

—ALMA WHITE, *Story of My Life*

It appears that Alma preached her first sermon at age thirty-one during the fall of 1893 in Erie, Colorado, where Kent had been transferred the prior June. Kent offered her his pulpit and she preached a sermon she entitled "Achan in the Camp." Although the story of Achan is in the Old Testament, Alma's topic was Christian holiness. She related: "I found the doctrine of holiness taught where I had never seen it before, in both the Old and the New Testament, and wanted to preach it to others and see them led into the experience."[24]

Sanctification had transformed Alma's personality, enabling her to overcome the timidity and fear of speaking that had kept her silent on earlier occasions. Alma spoke of sanctification as "the great event of my life, fitting me for the preaching of the gospel."[25] After her sanctification, Alma possessed "holy boldness,"[26] a characteristic that often accompanied the second work of grace. In order to retain sanctification, Alma believed, as did Phoebe Palmer, that testifying publicly was mandatory: "The Scripture says, 'Ye are my witnesses,' and I knew that in order to keep the experience of sanctification I should have to take a stand for the truth and give forth no uncertain sound."[27] Sanctification provided Alma with the power of the Holy Spirit, which gave her the courage to preach.

Alma had to overcome another obstacle before she could launch her preaching career. She had suffered from poor health for several years prior to her sanctification. Because doctors' prescriptions and advice had not helped, Alma decided that her only recourse was to rely on God to heal her. Many individuals involved in the Wesleyan/Holiness movement believed in divine healing. Some refused all medical care, whereas others, including Alma, professed that God could work in conjunction with doctors. Alma claimed healing by faith, just as she had claimed sanctification by faith, and reported: "There was no great or sudden change, but I was confident [God] had undertaken for me and that as my days, so should my strength be."[28] It is impossible to assess Alma's understanding of the extent of her healing. Perhaps her paraphrase of Deuteronomy 33:25 ("as your days, so is your strength") reflected a belief that God would fortify her daily in the event that divine healing did not result in completely restored health. In another account, she indicated that her healing was not instantaneous: "As time went on I could see a great improvement in my health."[29] Alma continued to speak of ailments that were similar to the ones she suffered prior to her sanctification, but she was able to persevere in her ministry despite them.

Alma's next opportunity to preach was at Pleasant View where Kent and other evangelists initiated a revival on November 13, 1893. The revival, on Kent's Erie circuit, had been underway for ten days with no conversions. The first night Alma attended, Kent allowed her to conduct the altar service after his sermon. Alma exhorted members of the congregation to come forward to the altar to pray. This, her first altar service, resulted in five persons seeking salvation and thirteen others praying for the experience of sanctification. Alma preached every night for the next three weeks.

Alma's niece Stella Mayfield watched Arthur and Ray while Alma traveled five miles each way to the Pleasant View revival. Alma justified her absences from home by claiming her duty to God superseded her parental obligations. Alma's activities illustrate the application of Phoebe Palmer's altar theology. Alma, like Phoebe, believed one must sacrifice everything on the altar of Christ, including one's family. God's work had top priority.[30] Rather than neglecting her sons, Alma was entrusting them to God's care. She missed her children when she traveled, but she was convinced the sacrifice was necessary to fulfill her calling to preach.

Following the Pleasant View revival, Alma received calls to hold revivals in school houses in neighboring areas. In the spring of 1894, she conducted a series of meetings in a rented hall at Lafayette, a coal-mining town four miles from Erie. This was her first "independent" meeting, conducted outside the auspices of the Methodist Episcopal church. Alma claimed that during the year she held revivals in various places, "with nearly two hundred converts."[31]

Despite the spiritual success on Kent's Erie circuit, or perhaps because of it, Stephen M. Merrill, the presiding bishop in 1894, assigned Kent to the Broomfield circuit for the coming year. Bishop Merrill was known for his opposition to the doctrine of sanctification. This appointment, without a parsonage or a church building, was normally given to a seminary student who conducted services in two schoolhouses. Alma construed the placement as an insult and an attempt to situate her and Kent in a location from which it would be difficult to reach upcoming revival engagements in the area around Erie, which was twelve miles from Broomfield. Kent served the Broomfield circuit for the coming year, but the couple circumvented the church hierarchy's intention by maintaining their residence in Erie.

Along with her initial evangelistic campaigns, Alma claimed responsibility for arranging most of the details of the first camp meeting sponsored by the Colorado Holiness Association, even though officially this was Kent's job as secretary of the organization. A camp meeting differed from a revival in that people came for several days and pitched tents and services were conducted several times throughout the day rather than just in the evening. Alma's assessment of her role in this group included an indictment of the spiritual condition of the other officers:

> Knowing that someone who actually had been sanctified would have to exert an energizing force back of the organization if anything were accomplished, I did all I could to see the work go forward and to keep my husband interested so that the business would not be neglected; and this was no small task.[32]

The Colorado Holiness Association was organized the summer of 1893 at a joint meeting of the People's Tabernacle and the Haymarket Mission, two holiness missions in Denver. The founding of this association paralleled the growth of the Wesleyan/Holiness movement nationally. Advocates of holiness doctrine formed regional groups that planned and supervised meetings devoted solely to the promotion of holiness. The first camp meeting was held in 1801 in Cane Ridge, Kentucky; the first holiness camp meeting was held in 1867 at Vineland, New Jersey.[33] Although the meetings were interdenominational, the leadership nationally, as well as in Colorado, was primarily Methodist.

The first camp meeting sponsored by the Colorado Holiness Association took place during the summer of 1894 at Herrings Grove near Pleasant View. Alma secured William Godbey, the pastor from Kentucky who was instrumental in her conversion, to serve as the speaker. By this time, Godbey had become one of the most well-known Wesleyan/Holiness evangelists in the country.[34] As with Alma, the experience of sanctification had signified an important milestone in his spiritual journey. Godbey testified: "Sanctification is a most notable epoch in my experience marking a radical revolution in my life."[35] Others observed the change in Godbey's preaching after his sanctification. One person noted that during the first fifteen years of his ministry, Godbey "was not remarkable as a pastor," but his sanctification in 1868 transformed him into "a flaming evangelist and one of the most successful revivalists of his day."[36] Godbey's presiding bishop had granted him the status of a connectional evangelist in 1884, allowing him the freedom to travel throughout the country rather than being restricted to one congregation or circuit.

Alma's mother arrived from Kentucky in time for the 1894 camp meeting at Herrings Grove. Both Mrs. Bridwell and Alma's brother Charles claimed sanctification at this meeting. Alma had convinced Charles to move to Colorado four years earlier to complete his ministerial training at the University of Denver. Charles had accepted his first pastorate at Black Hawk and Bald Mountain, Colorado, a few months prior to the camp meeting. Mrs. Bridwell lived with the Whites for two years and provided child care when Alma traveled to meetings.

On August 24, 1894, Alma and Charles embarked on an eleven-week revival trip to Montana and Idaho.[37] Kent filled Charles's pulpit during this time. Arthur traveled with Alma and Charles, but Ray stayed home with Alma's mother. Alma did not comment on the challenge of traveling with a five-year-old but merely mentioned that Arthur accompanied them. While in Montana Arthur perhaps stayed with Alma's brother Emery or her sisters Nora and Theresa West, who had moved there from Kentucky. Alma hated leaving two-year-old Ray at home and compared the separation to "taking a mother's heart from her body." Even though being away from Ray seemed "unbearable," she endured it because she believed she was fulfilling God's will and "it would be perilous to disobey."[38]

At Dillon, Montana, Rev. J. W. Tate of the Methodist Episcopal church vetoed the invitation his board and congregation had extended to Charles and Alma to conduct a revival at his church. Undaunted, the two ordered a large tent to be shipped from Denver and held services in it. Their relatives attended meetings in Dillon and also in Bannack. Before returning home, Alma and Charles led a revival in Pocatello, Idaho.

Kent joined Alma in Big Dry, Colorado, three weeks after she had begun a revival there during the fall of 1894. When the host pastor neglected to invite Kent to take part in the first evening service after his arrival, Alma suffered the consequences of the pastor's oversight. After the service, Kent found fault with her sermon until five o'clock in the morning. Alma implied that Kent resented her success as an evangelist: "From what he said, it seemed he felt he was not receiving the recognition that he should have."[39] Undissuaded by Kent's harangues, Alma continued preaching with subsequent revivals at Fort Lupton and at the Stone Schoolhouse seven miles from Erie.

During the annual conference in June 1895, Kent "located," or terminated his membership with the Colorado annual conference of the Methodist Episcopal church. As a located pastor, Kent retained his good standing in the conference but did not receive a regular assignment. The *Journal of the Methodist Episcopal Church in Colorado,* however, listed Kent as "supply" for 1895, which signified he was available to substitute for other pastors. According to the *Journal,* Kent accepted a temporary appointment during 1895, filling in for Charles again in Bald Mountain.[40]

Alma and Kent received national attention for their involvement in the 1895 camp meeting at Fort Collins. The *Guide to Holiness,* a national magazine promoting the doctrine of holiness, reported in its "Monthly Review" column that the Whites' preaching resulted in forty seekers coming to the altar to pray.[41] This is the only reference to Kent and Alma in the *Guide to Holiness,* which ceased publication in 1901. Prior to the camp meeting, Kent had threatened to leave Alma. Alma was vague about Kent's justification for abandoning the family:

"My husband began on the old score, complaining about different things."[42] Miranda ("Mother") Vorn Holz and Rebecca Grant, two well-known holiness workers, both pleaded with Kent to change his mind. Alma confessed her strategy: "I was satisfied that the only thing that would quiet him was to give him the opportunity to preach a time or two to the largest congregations, and so it proved."[43] Kent, however, claimed Mother Vorn Holz convinced him to stay. Alma's comment reveals the extent of her control over this camp meeting. Even though Kent was the secretary, she determined the program during the first few years of its existence.

Between July 1895 and the following summer, Alma and Kent answered requests to hold revivals in the Colorado cities of Longmont, Box Elder, Black Hollow, Holyoke, LaPorte, and Idaho Creek. Engagements usually lasted three or four weeks. Alma generally did not provide statistics, but she did relate that the tent at Longmont seated four hundred and "on Sunday evenings it was filled and hundreds stood on the outside."[44]

Alma's account of the Longmont revival sheds light on the supportive role of co-workers. Rebecca Grant, an African American, provided verbal encouragement and support by speaking out during the sermon: "Talk about Him, children, talk about Him," referring to Jesus.[45] Christians sought Grant's counsel both at her home in Denver and at her tent during camp meetings. Wesleyan/Holiness meetings were among the few places where people of different races joined in worship. Most other churches honored legal or informal Jim Crow policies that resulted in strict segregation. Another worker at the Longmont revival was Miranda Vorn Holz, a Wesleyan/Holiness evangelist from Kentucky. Even though she was seventy-two years old, Vorn Holz maintained an active schedule. She impressed Alma, who referred to her as a "mother in Israel."[46] This designation was one of honor denoting a woman's spiritual wisdom and maturity. The first mother in Israel was Deborah, the Old Testament judge who accompanied Barak into battle to assure his victory (Judges 4:4–5:15). Although Alma never spoke specifically of women who served as role models, her niece Gertrude Wolfram indicated the importance of Vorn Holz's example: "My aunt, through observing her and through association, came to know what the Bible means when it says 'Be filled with the Spirit,' and also the meaning of 'be instant in prayer,' and though Mother Von Holtz [*sic*] passed on, her example endured."[47]

METHODIST OPPOSITION

Women should be silent in the churches. For they are not permitted
to speak, but should be subordinate, as the law also says.
If there is anything they desire to know, let them ask their husbands
at home. For it is shameful for a woman to speak in church.

—1 CORINTHIANS *14:34–35*

Let a woman learn in silence with full submission.
I permit no woman to teach or to have authority over a man;
she is to keep silent.

—1 TIMOTHY *2:11–12*

Methodist clergy opposed Alma's preaching on three counts: her success as an evangelist, her preaching of holiness, and her sex. Alma believed the presiding elder and bishop had removed Kent from the Erie circuit in 1894 because they were envious of her successful revivals there. She suggested they were humiliated "to have a woman wield the sword of truth, when no recognition had been given her by ecclesiastical authorities, and she was supposed to have no place except that of servant."[48]

Initially, the Methodist Episcopal church had fostered the dissemination of holiness doctrine and played a prominent role in promoting holiness camp meetings. By the 1890s, however, some bishops, including Stephen Merrill and John Vincent, deplored the trend toward independent evangelistic activities in the Wesleyan/Holiness movement, which were unauthorized by them and outside their control. They became increasingly critical of holiness leaders, particularly outspoken ones such as Alma, who engaged in these activities. When one session of the 1894 conference meeting was opened for testimonies from those in attendance, Alma was the first person to rise to speak. Undaunted by Bishop Merrill, who "lowered his eyebrows and looked very gravely" at her, Alma testified to her experience of holiness.[49]

Two years later, Bishop Vincent, who opposed both the holiness doctrine and women preachers, presided over the Methodist conference in Leadville, Colorado. He took advantage of one devotional period to criticize women's ministry, reading from the book of Timothy, probably 1 Timothy 2:11–12, quoted above.

Pastors at the local level condemned women pastors as well.[50] Alma reported that "the enemy kept busy in the churches. The pastors said it was a woman's place to stay home and look after husband and children."[51] Such pastors accepted and promoted the popular notion of woman's sphere, which they invoked in an attempt to limit women's activities to the home. Alma recognized the myth of woman's sphere for what it was—a man-made contrivance. She rejected the rhetoric and renounced any boundaries imposed by the belief. Unintimidated by her detractors, Alma continued to preach, challenging the artificial restrictions imposed on women.

Because Methodist clergy also were active in the Colorado Holiness Association, the negative attitude toward women ministers infiltrated this group. Alma faced a groundswell of opposition to women preachers on the Fort Collins camp grounds at the second state holiness camp meeting in the early fall of 1895. She traced the problem to a Methodist minister (whom she did not name) who "charged women with being responsible for all of the crimes of the ages, from the sin of Mother Eve down to the present generation" and sought "to prove his assertions from the Scriptures."[52] In all likelihood, the speaker referred to the passages quoted above.

Alma's assessment of her situation was astute:

> If a woman received the baptism of the Holy Spirit and was called to preach she had to force every door open and be a suppliant at the feet of the pastors of the churches. Since they were not inclined to recognize her right to the ministry of God's word her only opportunity to preach was on the street corners or in the foreign missionary field. The holiness organization had done more for woman's ministry than all of the denominations, but there were so many carnal-minded people in connection with it that the opposition was sometimes very great.[53]

Alma was not surprised when the program committee for the 1897 camp meeting neglected to ask her to preach. During one evening service, Rev. J. A. DaFoe announced that four ministers would each speak five minutes. Kent was the fourth speaker, and when his turn came, he said a few words and then turned the pulpit over to Alma. Despite their unresolved marital difficulties, Kent was able, at times such as this, to rise above them. Alma took advantage of the opportunity and preached for fifty minutes. Some were appalled by her audacity, but Alma justified her conduct by the large number of seekers at the altar after her sermon.

The annual holiness camp meeting met at Island Grove Park near Greeley from August 28 to September 8, 1898. The program committee snubbed Alma again by refusing to issue her an invitation to preach even though she was a member of the Executive Council and on the Membership Committee of the Colorado Holiness Association, sponsor of the camp meeting. During one service, Alma received permission to describe her mission work, which at this time included missions in Denver, Colorado City, and Cheyenne, Wyoming. When people began contributing money, unsolicited, for the Cheyenne mission, the guest preacher intervened and halted the offering. This was the final straw for Alma:

> The way before me was now clear. . . . The vinegar and gall that was given me at this camp meeting was a blessing in disguise, and helped to prepare me for what the future would unfold. The barrier had been removed and there could be no possible room for regret in breaking away from those with whom I had been associated.[54]

Alma knew now that she would leave her denomination, but it would be another three years before she acted on this conviction.

The program committee overlooked Alma once more at the 1900 holiness camp meeting in Colorado Springs. Rev. J. A. DaFoe, chair of the committee, omitted Alma's name from handbills promoting the meeting. At one point when Kent was expected to preach, he looked to Alma, indicating that she should take his place. She did, thus circumventing the leaders' intention to keep her off the platform. Seth Rees, the guest speaker, endorsed Alma's message. Before the week was over, DaFoe made his way to Alma's tent with an official invitation to preach.

The next summer, DaFoe left Alma's name off handbills announcing the speakers for the annual Fourth of July Convention in Pleasant View. Alma had initiated the Fourth of July meetings and claimed that up to 1901 she had planned them as well as the camp meetings. This omission occurred despite the fact that she still served on the Executive Council of the Colorado Holiness Association. Although Alma recognized that holiness organizations fostered women's ministry more than most church groups or denominations, she realized negative attitudes toward women disposed some members to actively oppose her ministry. DaFoe's behavior reminded Alma that he and other Methodists did not value her ministry.

ALMA'S RESPONSE TO OPPOSITION

There are no scriptural grounds for prohibiting women
from preaching the Gospel or from leadership in the Church.
—ALMA WHITE, *Story of My Life*

Alma's defense of her right to preach corresponded to arguments developed by Wesleyan/Holiness advocates earlier in the nineteenth century. Proponents of women's ministry emphasized the fact that the passages from 1 Corinthians and 1 Timothy that Alma encountered in her early ministry were the only ones in the entire Bible that opponents of women ministers could produce to bolster their case. Supporters of women clergy pointed out that if these verses were literally applied by those denominations that prevented women from preaching, women would not be allowed to sing, pray, testify, teach, or write on religious subjects. Those who deferred to these passages as the final word in limiting women's involvement in the church were selective in their application of the proscriptions they believed the texts mandated.

Alma, like others, minimized the relevance of 1 Timothy 2:11–12 by claiming the passage was misapplied when it was invoked to prohibit women from preaching.[55] Instead, she focused her arguments on the context and original meaning of 1 Corinthians 14:34–35. Alma maintained that the intent of these two verses was to preserve order in the Corinthian congregation.[56] Women were disrupting the service by asking their husbands questions, so the prohibition was against asking questions, not against preaching. Alma further limited the application of the passage by contending that it applied only to the church in Corinth.[57]

Wesleyan/Holiness supporters of women clergy advised an examination of all New Testament writings relevant to the issue. They stressed that the prohibition of 1 Corinthians 14:34–35 could not have been intended to silence the religious utterances of Corinthian women because another verse in the same letter advised women to wear head coverings when they prayed or prophesied (1 Corinthians 11:5). Alma contended this verse endorsed women ministers, because in this context *prophecy* means *preach*.[58] Alma's perspective reflected the Wesleyan/Holiness consensus that these two terms are equivalent.[59]

After addressing the two passages misappropriated to prohibit women's ministry, Alma turned her attention to Acts 1 and 2, which recorded the events of Pentecost, the inauguration of the Christian church. The fact that Alma used the word *pentecostal* in the name of the church she ultimately founded illustrates her desire to conform to the practice of Pentecost. Pentecost was the beginning point of Wesleyan/Holiness vindications of women's ministry. Women's active role at Pentecost provided a precedent for future generations of women.

Prior to Pentecost, Jesus' followers gathered in Jerusalem to await "the promise of the Father," which Jesus described as follows: "But you will receive power when the Holy Spirit has come upon you; and you will be my witnesses in Jerusalem, in all Judea and Samaria, and to the ends of the earth" (Acts 1:8). Alma observed that the promise and divine commission in this verse embraced believers of both sexes.[60] When the appointed time came, all the followers assembled in the upper room were filled with the Holy Spirit and began to speak as the Spirit gave them utterance (Acts 2:4). The Holy Spirit filled men and women alike, showing no discrimination. Peter vindicated women's ministry to the crowds gathered in Jerusalem on the day of Pentecost by explaining that they were fulfilling the Old Testament prophecy of Joel: "In the last days it will be, God declares, that I will pour out my Spirit upon all flesh, and your sons and your daughters shall prophesy, and your young men shall see visions, and your old men shall dream dreams" (Acts 2:17–18). The account of Pentecost documents women's involvement in ministry in the early church. Alma concluded one discussion of Pentecost by claiming that the fulfillment of Joel's prophecy "forever settles the question as to women's ministry."[61]

Galatians 3:28 also bolstered the biblical case for women preachers: "There is no longer Jew or Greek, there is no longer slave or free, there is no longer male and female; for all of you are one in Christ Jesus." Alma, and others before and after her, quoted this verse extensively in the demand for the inclusion of women in ministry. To her, it demonstrated that "in the gospel dispensation both men and women have the privilege of expounding the Word of God and of teaching it to others."[62] B. T. Roberts, founder of the Free Methodist church (a Wesleyan/Holiness denomination), urged that those verses used in an attempt to oppose women preachers should be measured against the standard of Galatians 3:28: "Make this the KEY TEXT upon this subject, and give to other passages such a construction as will make them agree with it, and all is harmony."[63]

Along with the story of Pentecost in Acts and Galatians 3:28, Alma's argument included a litany of women in the New Testament as well as the Old Testament who served as models for women in ministry. Turning to the Old Testament, Alma mentioned Deborah, the judge and military strategist; Queen Esther, who risked her life to save her people; and Miriam, who helped lead the Hebrews out of bondage in Egypt.[64] In the New Testament, Alma identified Anna, a devout prophet who announced Jesus' mission when his parents brought him to the temple shortly after his birth for the ritual ceremony of purification.[65] The woman of Samaria, the first woman to proclaim the good news of Christ, was often the topic of Alma's sermons, because this unnamed woman illustrated God's approval of women's ministry.[66] After meeting Jesus at the well, the Samaritan woman whom Alma labeled a "New Covenant Preacher" shared Jesus' message with other people in her town.[67] The events surrounding Jesus' death and resurrection provided additional evidence favoring women in ministry. Jesus chose Mary Magdalene to proclaim the news of his resurrection. Alma observed: "Woman was last at the cross and first at the tomb, and was the first to herald the glad tidings of the risen Christ."[68] The phrase "last at the cross, first at the tomb" is an adaptation of the last line of a four-line poem quoted frequently in biblical analyses of women's rights:

> *Not she with traitorous lips her Savior stung,*
> *Not she denied him with unholy tongue.*
> *She, whilst apostles shrunk could danger brave;*
> *Last at the cross, and earliest at the grave.*[69]

Among the authors who quoted this stanza to illustrate women's faithfulness to Christ were Catherine Booth, cofounder of the Salvation Army, and Phoebe Palmer.

In addition to women in the Gospels, Alma documented the ministry of women in the early church. Philip had four daughters who prophesied (Acts 21:8).[70] Romans 16 mentions ten women, including the minister Phoebe; Priscilla, who was a co-laborer with Paul; and the apostle Junia.[71]

Alma believed the Bible was her strongest defense against those who disapproved of her ministry: "If I could not prove by the Word of God that women have as good a right to preach as men, I would have but little use for the Bible."[72] She quoted Scripture passages that supported women's expanded role in the church and criticized her opponents' faulty interpretation of verses. Attempts to silence Alma by appeals to the Bible proved fruitless.

MINISTRY IN DENVER

The time had come for us to move from Erie. We had lived there
for three years and I had held meetings in schoolhouses, halls,
and some churches, for miles around, and the ground had all been covered.
It was time for a new departure in the work. It was also made clear
that we should locate in Denver.

—ALMA WHITE, *Story of My Life*

By early summer of 1896, Alma was ready to tackle new territory. Undeterred by opposition to her ministry, she set her sights on Denver, and the family moved to a rented home adjacent to Lincoln Park in west Denver. Without a regular preaching assignment, Kent was free to move.

A key attraction of the Denver home was its double parlor where, within two weeks after moving, Alma initiated a Thursday afternoon holiness meeting. Modeled after Phoebe Palmer's famous Tuesday Meeting for the Promotion of Holiness held in her home in New York City, the informal meetings consisted of testimonies, singing, and prayer. By 1892, there were 354 meetings for the promotion of holiness, each patterned after the New York Tuesday Meeting.[73]

Tent and street meetings, mission services, and prayer meetings soon occupied Alma's time in Denver. Within six months after moving there, Alma reported that four hundred people had experienced salvation at services she sponsored.[74] Hattie Livingston, an evangelist affiliated with the Wesleyan Methodist Church (a Wesleyan/Holiness denomination), loaned Alma her Gospel Tabernacle, a tent Alma pitched on June 16 at a central location in Denver. Miranda Vorn Holz assisted at the six-week meeting by praying with persons seeking conversion. Other workers conducted street meetings on two or more street corners prior to the evening services. Every afternoon, workers held prayer meetings.

The Whites established an independent mission on July 7, 1896, near Seventeenth and Market streets in Denver, calling it the Pentecostal Home Mission. Mr. Denton, who had attended the first holiness camp meeting in 1894, offered the second floor of his business establishment for use as a mission hall. Miranda Vorn Holz agreed to oversee the mission. Vorn Holz, who had already worked previously with Alma in several revivals and camp meetings, had extensive experience in evangelism and mission work, primarily in the Midwest.[75] During an earlier visit to Denver in 1893, she had conducted meetings for two weeks each at the Haymarket Mission and the People's Tabernacle. Vorn Holz described Market Street as one of the worst streets in Denver, crowded with prostitutes and saloons.[76] Assisted by Alma's mother, Vorn Holz began praying on the street corner to attract an audience for the indoor services. Police stopped the outdoor prayer meetings when a saloon proprietor complained that the praying interfered with his business. Under Vorn Holz's supervision, there were 225 conversions at the mission during the summer of 1896.

Urban holiness missions thrived in Denver during the 1890s, reflecting a national pattern. Tom Uzzell pastored the People's Tabernacle, a mission offering a broad program designed to meet the needs of its poor constituency.[77] It sponsored night schools, kindergartens, a free medical dispensary, a legal aid clinic, and an employment agency, and offered hot showers at its facility. Rev. A. C. Peck, who superintended the Haymarket Mission, had asked Kent and Alma to work in his mission with the stipulation that they tone down their preaching on holiness. He specifically requested that they refrain from using the word *sanctification* because it aroused so much opposition. Predictably, Alma refused to accept the offer, given Peck's terms. In her own mission, she answered to no one. Alma exulted in her freedom: "No one could shackle me now."[78]

The expansion of Alma's ministry from evangelistic work to missions paralleled the pattern of development among holiness groups throughout the country at this time. Alma, like many holiness evangelists, established independent missions after participating in ecumenical holiness camp meetings and revivals. Converts staffed the city missions, which operated on the "faith line." Rather than publicizing their needs, mission workers relied on unsolicited donations. In Alma's case, converts from rural areas surrounding Denver donated food to the mission.

The competition between missions in Denver accelerated on January 1, 1897, when St. James Methodist Church opened Peniel Mission a few blocks from one of Alma's missions. (She had established a second mission by this time.) To make matters worse, Alma's brother Charles agreed to be in charge of the Peniel Mission. Although not revealing Charles's motivation for his defection, Alma confessed that his decision to manage the mission hurt her deeply. Rhoda Wertheim, who had assisted Alma at revivals in Erie and Big Dry, Colorado, also joined the ranks of Peniel Mission workers and lured Alma's followers away from her missions. Alma criticized Rev. C. B. Allen, pastor of St. James Church, for stealing her converts: "With a broad smile and a warm hand shake he beguiled those for whom I had suffered and travailed in birth, the most of whom had been reached through the street preaching." Alma castigated Allen and other Methodist pastors in Denver who "were too proud to go into the byways and hedges and fulfill the divine commission in compelling the people to come in." According to Alma, the pastors in Denver expected her and her staff to do the hard work, after which they could move in and "reap the results."[79]

Along with her commitments in Denver, Alma remained involved in the Colorado Holiness Association camp meetings. W. B. Godbey traveled West for the 1896 camp meeting in Fort Collins. Amanda Smith, a prominent African-American evangelist in the holiness movement, attended the fourth annual meeting at Plum's Crossing (near Pleasant View) in 1897. Despite her reputation, Alma was not impressed with Smith and accused her of spending all her time raising money for an orphanage for African-American children, which she opened two years later in Harvey, Illinois.

A milestone in Alma's ministry was the distribution of thirty-five hundred copies of the first edition of the *Pentecostal Mission Herald.* Dated December 1897, the twelve-page paper provided news of two missions Alma had established in Leadville and Cripple Creek, Colorado. The charity department at the Denver mission had distributed 990 garments, with 738 going to children. The paper also printed several religious articles, a song Alma had written, and Kent's report on the activities of the Colorado Holiness Association.

Alma had persuaded a reluctant Kent to edit the paper but was unable to motivate him to publish it on a regular basis. The next issue rolled off the presses in December 1898, and the third appeared belatedly in January 1902. Alma realized that a regular publication would add legitimacy to her ministries. Newspapers established an identity for Wesleyan/Holiness groups and provided news for geographically scattered supporters.

The next stage of organizational development in Alma's ministry was the establishment of a training school for her workers. Alma called a planning meeting on November 3, 1898, which forty-five supporters attended. They decided to operate the school by faith, and soon money came in to cover rent and other expenses. Alma's first training school opened on February 1, 1899, at 818 Twenty-second Street in Denver, relocating later that spring to a seventeen-room house at 2348 Champa Street, which had formerly been a homeopathic hospital. The school, named the Pentecostal Mission Home, accommodated forty persons and began accepting students after the move to Champa Street. Its purpose was to educate young workers in doctrine and method, providing room and board so they could devote all their efforts to missionary and evangelistic work rather than having to worry about supporting themselves as well. Alma's followers from rural areas around Denver continued to support her ministries by providing supplies for the home.

It is impossible to determine the extent of Kent's role in the various ministries initiated by Alma after they moved to Denver. He repeated his threat to leave the family after the first mission opened. Alma said he was in "an unhappy mood" and "it seemed he felt he was not receiving the recognition that he should have."[80] She provided no other details. One of Kent's concerns may have been a fear of jeopardizing his standing in the Methodist Episcopal church, whose leaders perceived independent missions as hostile competition. Yet according to Vorn Holz's account of the first mission, Kent rather than Alma had asked her to work there. This seems to indicate that Kent played a prominent role in the early leadership. On the other hand, Kent seldom attended the street meetings and would cancel mission services when Alma was away. Kent also opposed the idea of a training school. Alma noted that his loyalty to Methodism stood in the way: "My husband had never shown any disposition to hazard anything that would bring him into disfavor with church officials."[81]

In June 1899, Alma and Kent and their sons traveled to Butte, Montana, to establish a mission. City officials denied their request for a permit to hold open-air meetings, but they conducted them anyway as a means to publicize the mission. For some reason they were not arrested. They also promoted the mission through door-to-door calling and distribution of religious tracts.

Back in Denver, Alma closed the mission she had operated on Larimer Street for two and a half years and conducted nightly services during the summer in a large tent pitched at Twenty-third and California streets.

Alma's ministry had expanded dramatically since her initial preaching efforts in Erie and Pleasant View. By the turn of the twentieth century, she had held revivals throughout Colorado and had traveled to Montana and Idaho. She calculated that she had conducted three thousand services between 1896 and 1900.

AN UNPREDICTABLE PARTNER

My strong battle was under our own roof. How to withstand
the opposition coming from my husband was the greatest problem.
The antagonism on his part, which was unceasing, resulted in
weakening my physical vitality, undermining my work for the Lord.
—ALMA WHITE, *Story of My Life*

Alma's first years of preaching were interspersed with periods of cooperation and conflict with Kent. From the start, Kent had opposed

Alma's symbolic interpretation of Scripture and rejected her contention that typologies throughout the Bible confirmed the holiness doctrine. He claimed that no Bible commentaries would support her hermeneutics. Kent had criticized Alma's first sermon in Erie in 1893 and, on another occasion, had challenged her symbolic application of the story of Jonah in the big fish.[82] Contrary to Alma's interpretation, it was clear to Kent that Jonah's encounter with the fish did not illustrate the two works of grace. Undaunted by Kent's disapproval, Alma added fuel to the fire by offering even more typologies in her preaching at Pleasant View during the fall of 1893. As this revival progressed, Kent's criticism increased; sometimes he attacked Alma all the way home, a five-mile drive, and prolonged the quarrel far into the night.

Less than one year later, Alma bemoaned Kent's critical stance toward her preaching:

> As I labored on from day to day and the work enlarged on my hands he became more bold in his denunciations and criticisms, sometimes assuming the attitude of an anxious and affectionate husband who wished to keep me from going too near the precipice. It was more difficult to withstand him under this guise than when he was openly hostile.[83]

In the spring of 1895, Alma and Kent worked together at a revival in her brother Charles's church at Bald Mountain. Although Alma claimed Kent's antagonism was "unceasing," there were periods of intermittent cooperation. Things were going well until Alma preached on the parable of the prodigal son who demanded his share of the family inheritance and then squandered it. The son returned home, hoping to be hired as a servant, but his father welcomed him back into the family and celebrated his return with a party. Alma elaborated on how this story illustrated the two works of grace: "I showed how the kiss of forgiveness [when the son returns to his father's house] symbolizes the first work of grace and the putting on of the best robe and feasting on the fatted calf, the second work of grace, or sanctification."[84] Predictably, Kent challenged her interpretation because he was convinced the parable had nothing to do with sanctification. Alma worried about the effects their argument might have on the congregation: "It was his custom to speak loudly. I felt quite sure the people in the house had heard him and I feared it would be told among the parishioners the next day."[85] Sometimes Alma closed revivals early when Kent began challenging her. She felt she could not wage a battle simultaneously on two fronts because it required too much energy to withstand Kent's verbal attacks and preach at the same time.

Notwithstanding his threat to leave the family prior to the 1895 camp meeting, Kent accompanied Alma on a revival campaign following the camp meeting to nearby cities, including Box Elder and Black Hollow. Apparently, they temporarily patched up their differences. Against Alma's wishes, Kent organized a Methodist class meeting with converts from Box Elder. Alma feared that when a Methodist pastor took over her converts, she would lose contact with them. This proved to be the case. Alma preached at the Black Hollow meetings while Kent visited and talked with people. In light of the tensions in the relationship, one wonders how Kent and Alma divided the duties. It is hard to imagine Kent accepting this arrangement, yet several months later when he was invited to work in a meeting at Gold Hill, he refused to go without Alma. At times Kent was able to overlook theological differences and collaborate with Alma. Despite misgivings about working in a Methodist charge and feeling that her efforts would be better rewarded elsewhere, Alma reluctantly agreed to accompany Kent to Gold Hill to, as she put it, "keep peace in the family."[86]

Kent began a series of meetings in the Peter Brown schoolhouse (five miles east of Greeley) on January 7, 1898. At first Alma was not asked to help. After ten days, Kent wrote, begging Alma to come at once because "the meeting was blocked," meaning no one was seeking salvation or sanctification at the altar. Alma responded to Kent's plea and reported that things soon changed: "A break came that turned the whole front of the house into an altar of prayer, and during the next ten days the country was aflame with the revival spirit and many sought and found the Lord."[87] Alma's effectiveness as a preacher sometimes enabled Kent to overlook her faulty biblical interpretation and cooperate with her in revival work. The revival spread across the river to Kersey where services were held during February and March. Against Alma's wishes, Kent organized a Methodist church at the first location, which became known as Bethel, and established a Methodist class at Kersey. Alma was clear about Kent's rationale for his action. He was "trying to seek the favor of the Church officials and build up a reputation for himself as the result of my labors."[88] The Methodist Episcopal conference established the Greeley circuit, consisting of Bethel and Kersey, and placed it under Kent's supervision for nearly two years after the revival.

On March 22, 1898, the revival shifted to Lucerne (eight miles north of Greeley). Kent's presiding elder hoped that a Methodist church would result from these meetings, as had been the case in Bethel and Kersey, and that the community church already in existence would affiliate with the Methodists. Alma, who was not interested in contributing to the growth of Methodism, had resisted collaborating with Kent at this revival, but Kent insisted that she accompany him. When Alma decided she was ready to return to Denver, Kent subjected her to a wakeful night arguing against her leaving. Their hosts overheard the discussion and Alma reported that "the story went forth that the preacher and his wife were disagreeing over the services and that the inmates of the house had been kept awake the entire night as a result."[89] After praying about the matter, Alma concluded:

> The Lord clearly spoke to me telling me there would be no revival at this place, and that my labors should not be used to help further the selfish interests of the officials of Methodism who had no sympathy with me or the Gospel that I preached, except as my services could be used to advance their worldly ambitions.[90]

Alma apparently left Lucerne, defying Kent's wishes.

During the summer of 1899, friction erupted between Alma and Kent in Butte, Montana, where the family had gone to establish a mission. One evening, Kent objected to Alma's sermon on the apostasy of the modern church and publicly challenged her in front of the congregation rather than waiting until after the service. Alma was humiliated. Kent continued the discussion far into the night, and the next morning he picked up where he had left off. Also, Alma was displeased with Kent because he had begun cooperating with the Methodists in Butte and agreed with them that her views on holiness and the condition of modern churches were extreme. Alma did not provide specifics in this instance, but one can understand why the Methodists were upset, given her low opinion of Methodism. For instance, she compared the Methodist church to "a dead mother wrapped in grave clothes, the fumes from the putrefying corpse stifling everyone that came in contact with it."[91]

When Alma decided it was time for the family to leave Butte, she arranged for missionary workers to assume the leadership of the mission. Kent, though, chose to stay. Alma returned to Denver with Arthur and Ray, arriving December 14, 1899. She wrote Kent, "insisting on his coming home, but there was no inclination on his part to do so."[92] Kent belatedly arrived in Denver almost three months later, on March 10, 1900.

By this phase in her ministry, Alma considered Kent her assistant rather than an equal partner. Alma revealed at one point that she did not expect Kent to attend all her services "but it was a great help to have him present occasionally to preach or take part."[93] During their courtship, Alma and Kent had both assumed she would perform the traditional role of a minister's wife and support Kent in his ministry. Now the roles were reversed, but Kent never adjusted to the change.

FOUNDING THE PENTECOSTAL UNION

The author drank from the Methodist brook,
but when the waters became stagnant and the odor of death ensued
she had to remove the rubbish so the water of life
might break forth in another place, or perish.

—ALMA WHITE, *Gospel Truth*

Kent's obscure church placement in Broomfield, Colorado, in 1894 had been one early factor that helped unloose Alma's ties to Methodism. Reacting to the church's negative treatment of Kent, she confessed:

> I had not only died to the Methodist Church, but to all other denominations that had ceased to contend for the faith that was once delivered to the saints. I saw that I could no longer be under the leadership of these denominations and keep the anointing of the Holy Spirit upon my soul.[94]

Alma's allegiance to Methodism diminished, but Kent maintained his connection to the church.

Alma's disillusionment with Methodism was exacerbated by the shabby treatment she had endured from its male clergy. From outright opposition to more subtle strategies such as being "overlooked" for preaching assignments during camp meetings, it was clear to Alma that her ministry was unappreciated. She commented on the consequence of persistent disapproval of her ministry by leaders in the Colorado Holiness Association:

> The opposition that I now had to meet under the cloak of holiness was fiercer than it had been in the Methodist Church but it finally led to my complete liberation from entanglements with both the church and the Holiness Association.[95]

By the fall of 1900, Alma believed the time had come to sever her denominational ties and organize her own church. According to Alma:

> People were attending our services in greater numbers than ever before, and great manifestations of God's power were continually in our midst. Clergymen and others prominent in Christian work were often in attendance, and it was evident that a nucleus was being formed for enlargement. There was a greater expression of confidence among our patrons and a deepening in spiritual things. I had held meetings in many places in Colorado, and opened missions and held revivals in adjoining states, and a new epoch had been reached.[96]

Alma was ready to declare her freedom from Methodism. When she began mentioning the possibility of establishing a separate religious group, Kent often threatened to leave with Ray and go to the Pacific Coast. Miranda Vorn Holz visited during the fall and, despite Kent's opposition, encouraged Alma to act on her convictions and form an independent organization.

Like others in the Wesleyan/Holiness movement, Alma came to the conclusion that the Methodist Episcopal church had compromised with the world and no longer represented authentic Christianity. She was blunt in her assessment: "To hold meetings and turn the converts over to the old denominations was like feeding lambs to wolves." Alma resented others "who were unwilling to bear the weight of a feather in the interest of souls" but had no qualms profiting from her labors by proselytizing her converts. Alma concluded, "There could be no means of defense without a new organization."[97] Her mind was made up, but she hesitated to take the final step toward denominational formation. More than likely, Kent's continuing allegiance to Methodism contributed to Alma's caution. She realized that any move to leave Methodism would antagonize him.

Alma attended the General Holiness Assembly held at the First Methodist Church in Chicago, May 3–13, 1901. Leading Wesleyan/Holiness workers, ninety men and twenty-five women, issued the call to the assembly. In a letter written from Chicago during the assembly, Alma noted the recognition she received at the meeting and compared it to the negative reception she had suffered in Colorado. She addressed the assembly twice, giving brief testimonies on Sunday and Tuesday, and she prayed Wednesday afternoon. Leaders consulted her regarding the constitution they were preparing. This was Alma's first exposure to the Wesleyan/Holiness movement at the national level. She claimed later that she was not impressed: "It is needless to say that it was spiritually dead and was of very little interest to me."[98] Although the prevalence of Methodists undoubtedly clouded Alma's perceptions of the meeting, it seems that the passing of time also contributed to her negative assessment.

People attended the assembly for various reasons. Prominent Methodists intended to contain the Wesleyan/Holiness movement within Methodism. They were concerned about holiness people, such as those in the Church of God (Anderson, Indiana), who were urging individuals to come out of their denominational churches and affiliate with them. Others, such as C. B. Jernigan, who traveled from Texas, came hoping that the conference would result in the organization of a national holiness church.[99] Both groups were disappointed. A national church did not emerge from the meeting, but neither were Methodists able to retain all the holiness advocates within their ranks. Alma was among those who ultimately abandoned Methodism.

A rival meeting, held simultaneously in the chapel of the same church hosting the General Holiness Assembly, appealed more to Alma. Its worship style was more lively and its participants were less loyal to Methodism. It was sponsored by the Metropolitan Church Association, a holiness group based in Chicago that had organized in 1894 following a revival at the Metropolitan Methodist Church. The two meetings symbolized the tension within the Wesleyan/Holiness movement nationally—the desire to confine holiness believers within Methodism versus the formation of spinoff groups. Although Alma shifted her attention to the rival meeting, she was at the General Holiness Assembly long enough to be listed on the assembly roll with 218 other delegates and to be appointed on Friday morning by Rev. C. J. Fowler, the president of the assembly, to the Committee on the Publication of the Proceedings of the Assembly. In light of her subsequent involvement at the Metropolitan Church Association meeting, she probably did not follow through on this commitment.

Alma's friend Seth Rees attended the Metropolitan Church Association services, as did Martin Wells Knapp, a Wesleyan/Holiness revivalist and former Methodist Episcopal pastor from Cincinnati, who advised that Christians would have to leave the old denominations in order to maintain favor with God.[100] His sentiments corresponded with Alma's, confirming her belief that there was no hope within Methodism for true Christianity to flourish. Alma's own thinking along these lines predisposed her to prefer this meeting.

Speakers at the Chicago meeting sponsored by the Metropolitan

Church Association fostered Alma's separatist tendencies. They reinforced her own conviction that her ministry could best proceed if she severed all ties to Methodism. Back in Denver, her plan to establish her own religious society gathered momentum, with many who attended her services supporting the idea of an independent church. Not surprisingly, Kent objected. On December 29, 1901, Alma and fifty charter members formally organized her mission work, naming it the Pentecostal Union Church. Kent was not present at the organizational meeting. It appears that Alma arranged his absence in order to avoid a possible conflict over the matter.

Pentecostal was a popular term in the Wesleyan/Holiness movement, referring to the gift of the Holy Spirit bestowed on Jesus' followers at Pentecost. Many equated sanctification with this gift. Alma's choice of words indicated the centrality of holiness in her doctrine. Today, *pentecostal* refers to the belief in glossolalia, or speaking in tongues, and the Pentecostal movement embraces those individuals and groups that practice glossolalia. Alma's adoption of *pentecostal* reflects the earlier understanding of the term, before it was associated with speaking in tongues.

Organizing a separate religious group placed Alma among the ranks of the "come-outers." Her separation from the Methodist Episcopal church mirrored a national pattern. In its infancy, the Wesleyan/Holiness movement organized associations that sponsored camp meetings. The next phase of organizational development was the establishment of interdenominational missions that in some cases resulted in the formation of independent churches. Between 1893 and 1907 the Wesleyan/Holiness movement generated at least twenty-five holiness sects in the United States, one of which was Alma's Pentecostal Union.[101] Founders of new holiness churches such as the Pentecostal Union or the Pentecostal Church of the Nazarene sought to reestablish the New Testament gospel that they contended Methodism had abandoned. Alma stressed: "I am not advocating a new religion. It is the old-time religion."[102]

Alma's conviction that Methodism had departed from true Christianity was a significant factor in her decision to found the Pentecostal Union. Another reason was Methodism's refusal to ordain women or affirm their right to preach. Alma explicitly connected the expectation of ordination to her decision to form the Pentecostal Union:

> Seventeen years before [in 1887], I was wrapped in the old ecclesiastical mantle and ready to lay my life down in sacrifice on the altar of

the Methodist Church; but she made no provision for me to preach
the Gospel and therefore it was in the mind of God to establish a
new, soul-saving institution where equal opportunities should be
given to both men and women to enter the ministry.[103]

Alma's ordination occurred on March 16, 1902, during a ten-day
revival led by Seth and Frida Rees in Denver. Although still in the
Friends church at this time, Seth Rees was supportive of independent
churches. Alma and four others, three men and one woman, were
ordained at the same service. Seth and Frida Rees, Charles Bridwell,
Methodist pastor J. A. Lemen, and Kent White (apparently reconciled
to his wife's abdication from Methodism) signed Alma's certificate of
ordination. Ordination signified the final milestone in Alma's liberation from the Methodist Episcopal church: "For years, as a preacher of
the Gospel, I had suffered humiliating handicaps on account of my sex,
but this achievement broke my chains in a measure and liberated me,
placing diamonds in my crown of rejoicing."[104] Now thirty-nine years
old, Alma achieved professional recognition for a calling she had
received twenty-three years earlier. As an ordained member of the
clergy, Alma could perform the sacraments and marry couples. Practi-
cally speaking, she could save money by traveling to evangelistic
engagements on reduced railroad clergy fares.

Alma incorporated the Pentecostal Union with the Colorado secretary of state on March 19, 1902. Surprisingly, Kent had overcome his
initial misgivings and relinquished his Methodist clergy credentials
five days prior to this date. Up until then, he had maintained staunch
opposition to Alma's plans. Alma observed that Kent "was usually in
an antagonistic mood on questions pertaining to an independent organization."[105] At a Thursday afternoon holiness meeting on January 19,
1902, Kent argued against Alma's position that the group should
remain independent of other churches. No clues have been discovered
to shed light on what changed Kent's mind. At this point, Kent sided
with Alma. She later claimed that his support was inconsistent:
"[Kent] never was fully in harmony with us, although at times his
assistance in the various enterprises was much appreciated."[106]

3
Development of Ministry

HOLY JUMPING AND THE PENTECOSTAL UNION

The Lord has launched out {the Pentecostal Union}
to keep true religion alive on the earth
in the midst of so much latter day apostasy.
—ALMA WHITE, *Story of My Life*

Alma supervised approximately forty mission pastors and evangelists at the founding of the Pentecostal Union. She had established missions in four states whose superintendents, for the most part, had completed training at her school in Denver. Things initially looked promising, yet more than half of the charter members soon defected. Alma did not record reasons for the desertions. Alma's mother, who maintained her alliance with the Colorado Holiness Association, was among those who opposed Alma's decision to establish an independent church. Alma provided a home for her mother in Denver, but the two remained estranged. Alma observed: "My worst foes have been among my own kinsfolk."[1]

Despite strong opposition and the depletion in her ranks, Alma persevered. With the coming of summer in 1902, she erected a tent with a capacity of two hundred at Eighteenth and Stout streets in Denver. The "joyful demonstrations" of the worship leaders and the congregation during the services drew the attention of reporters, whose subsequent descriptions of the lively worship drew large crowds to the tent to see the "jumpers," their nickname for Pentecostal Union members. Reporters assumed Alma's "holy jumping" was unique. In the United States, however, the practice of jumping as an expression of religious praise goes back at least to the first Great Awakening when Sarah Edwards, wife of Jonathan Edwards, experienced a spiritual moment so intense that she leaped with joy.[2] "Acrobatic Christianity" also exhibited itself during revivals at the beginning of the nineteenth century in Kentucky and Tennessee.[3] Alma had initially observed jumping at a Salvation Army service in Denver in 1888. Other contemporary Wesleyan/Holiness groups, such as the Free Methodists, also engaged in jumping. Rather than claiming historical precedence for the lively worship style, Alma referred her critics to Luke 6:22–23, where Jesus encouraged his followers to leap for joy when they were persecuted. Alma paraphrased "leap for joy" as to "jump up and down many times."[4] Alma had implemented the more informal worship style after observing jumping at the Metropolitan Church Association meeting in Chicago the prior summer.

Alma's tent meeting also attracted notice from nearby neighbors. Dismayed by the noise, twenty-eight of them petitioned the mayor in August, asking him not to renew the tent permit. Coroner W. P. Horan, whose business was diagonally across the street from the tent, contended that "the noise made by the 'Jumpers' in their religious ecstasies was so great that it kept his attendants from sleeping at night and almost disturbed the repose of his customers."[5] Despite the complaints of the residents and business owners in the immediate neighborhood, the mayor, swayed by counterpetitions filed by the Pentecostal Union, renewed the permit, allowing the tent to remain in place throughout the month of August.

Alma bought land in Denver on Champa Street, culminating the transaction on September 20, 1902. This was the first of many property purchases Alma successfully negotiated for the Pentecostal Union. People donated money for the down payment, including one young man who pledged one thousand dollars. After he withdrew five hundred dollars from his account, his father refused to release the other five hundred from the bank, convinced that his son was suffering from "religious mania."[6] Eventually, the money became available for Alma's use.

Construction of the Champa Street building stopped whenever funds were unavailable, so Alma was continually burdened with the responsibility of raising money. Alma also believed her presence was required to keep the workers motivated: "Some of the younger workers would often shirk their duties, and needed a firm hand to hold them steady, and it was necessary for me to be among them the most of the time." Kent continued to be an unpredictable ally. Later in the year, when Alma was overwhelmed with money concerns relating to loans on the lots, she desired Kent's aid but reported that he "was depressed in spirit and not disposed to give the help" she needed.[7]

In the meantime, Alma's followers added street parades to their repertoire of activities guaranteed to draw a crowd to their services. On February 8, 1903, Denver police arrested fifteen Pentecostal Union members for disturbing the peace. They had marched down Seventeenth Street from Champa to Larimer Street to the beat of a bass drum, waving handkerchiefs and carrying banners proclaiming religious slogans. A newspaper article the next day described the scene, claiming "there was much yelling and jumping," which frightened horses.[8] Police at the scene of the arrest offered a more graphic account: "They would jump three or four feet into the air, alternatively shouting religious sentiments and giving vent to unearthly screeches of no articulate form."[9] The marchers, under the leadership of Della Huffman, stated that the goal of their activity was to attract a large crowd. Once people gathered, the marchers would lead them to an indoor service. Their strategy worked; police reported that five hundred people were following this particular parade. Police escorted the Pentecostal Union marchers into a patrol wagon which carried them to jail where they continued singing and jumping. Rather than keeping them overnight, Police Chief Armstrong released the marchers when they promised to show up in court the next day. The Jumpers appeared in court on February 9 waving banners announcing Holiness or Hell, Jesus Is Coming, and Prepare to Meet Thy God. They were never ones to miss an opportunity to evangelize. Alma acted as counsel for the accused. Before releasing them, Judge Thomas lectured the group and told them he did not want to see them in his courtroom again. Undeterred, the marchers decided to parade again. They were arrested once more and, this time, spent the night in jail, except for Arthur and Ray who were released because they were minors.

Alma's ministry during 1903 extended beyond Colorado. During April and May, she conducted services at Omaha and Lincoln, Nebraska, as well as Dillon and Butte, Montana. Her father, who had moved to Dillon, attended the services there along with Aunt Eliza Mason. Alma recounted that twenty-five of her relatives had moved from Kentucky to Montana and lived in Beaverhead County, where she had taught as a young woman. Although she did not state the cause for the mass migration, her relatives probably made the move for economic reasons.

Back in Denver, police arrested Pentecostal Union marchers again on November 22, 1903. This time Kent, ignoring police instructions to remain in front of the Pentecostal Union building, had led a parade of twenty-four up Sixteenth Street, the main street in Denver, without a permit. The judge fined the marchers twenty-five dollars each plus court costs, but they chose the alternative of two weeks in jail. They served one night of their sentence before Alma succeeded in persuading the mayor to intervene and release them. Alma said her heart was "crushed and bleeding" to see Kent in jail, but she believed God had allowed this experience "to give him some necessary discipline and to check his ambition for the leadership he so much desired and for which he was not qualified."[10]

Other than defending her followers in court, Alma spent much of the fall of 1903 supervising the completion of the building at 1845 Champa Street. A convention beginning on January 8, 1904, signified the end of a seven-year interim of moving from one rented location to another. The participants met in the auditorium of the impressive brick structure, which measured 50 by 125 feet.[11] The auditorium on the first floor seated one thousand, and thirty-four bedrooms and several offices occupied the upper three floors. The basement consisted of a dining room, kitchen, laundry, press room, several storerooms, and a large classroom.

During the convention, which lasted two and a half weeks, the group ordained three women and two men, consecrated four missionaries, and licensed four people to preach. At one point, while the meetings were in session, one hundred newsboys pelted the building with rocks. The newsboys were upset because Alma had made disparaging comments about police officer John Askew for "conducting himself in a manner entirely unbecoming an officer of the law and acting much like an outlaw himself."[12] Askew, the officer who had arrested her followers the prior November, had smashed one of their banners during the arrest. Alma declared that his subsequent death was God's judgment for his behavior. Neighbors around the building came to Alma's defense. Although not condoning her tirade against Officer Askew, they charged that the police had incited the newsboys to harass the worshippers and then did not respond to calls for help. The neighbors threatened to report the incident to the fire and police board, demanding protection for the Pentecostal Union and themselves. The rock throwing stopped.

Alma's next encounter with the police occurred in Salt Lake City in April 1904. The chair of the board of trustees of a Nazarene church in Salt Lake City had invited Alma to come and hold services. This was followed by a request from the pastor to preach for a week. Before the week was out, the pastor had changed his mind and asked Alma to leave, probably because she had attacked another Nazarene church from his pulpit. The majority of the congregation voted to allow Alma to fulfill the original commitment. On Sunday morning, the pastor attempted to preach, claiming Alma's week was over. A local newspaper reported that her supporters "jumped on the benches and shouted until it was impossible for the meeting to be continued. A policeman was called and quiet was restored."[13] That evening, Alma persisted in leading the service. Opponents called police again, resulting in the arrest of Alma, one of her followers, and two other supporters. She was released, and the judge ultimately dismissed the case before it went to trial.

Following her brush with police in Salt Lake City, Alma conducted a revival in Los Angeles and attended camp meetings in Illinois and Texas during the summer of 1904 without incident. The first summer convention in the new Denver building started on September 8, 1904, and continued for eleven days. More than one thousand people crowded into the auditorium for the last service, including Alma's Aunt Eliza Mason from Montana and her father. Agreeing with Alma that Methodism had strayed from its roots, he had left the Methodist church and joined the Pentecostal Union, contributing short articles to the church paper. He lived at the Alma's Bible school until his death in 1907 at age eighty-two, and Alma testified that "he proved to be a blessing and an inspiration to all who knew him."[14] The support of Alma's father is in stark contrast to her mother's unceasing antagonism.

WORKING WITH THE BURNING BUSH

The Burning Bush and the Pentecostal Union
work together "in perfect harmony."

—ALMA WHITE

During its first several years, Alma's Pentecostal Union cosponsored revival meetings with the Metropolitan Church Association of Chicago. Alma had become acquainted with this group's leaders when she attended their meeting in Chicago the summer of 1901. The first cooperative venture for the Pentecostal Union and the Burning Bush, as the Metropolitan Church Association was popularly known, was a convention in Coliseum Hall, the largest auditorium in Denver, from July 25 to August 3, 1902. Duke Farson and E. L. Harvey, Burning Bush leaders, traveled to Denver for the convention. A reporter described one worship service during the convention: "When a man makes a point of jumping on the devil with both feet, coming down hard and grinding in with his heels, the thickest skinned devil will want to get out from under that platform and flee the wrath to come."[15] During the service, two men stood on chairs waving hand-kerchiefs, and E. L. Harvey cakewalked. Others whirled around with both hands up in the air or jumped up and down as if they were skipping rope.

Duke Farson had been an ordained minister in the Methodist Episcopal church, commissioned to do mission work in Chicago. He left his denomination to start his own church in Chicago in 1895. A well-known banker in Chicago, he financed the Burning Bush building there, which seated one thousand.[16] It might be assumed that the Burning Bush with its longer history and stronger financial base underwrote the revival, but this was not the case. The evangelists from Chicago offered their services free, but offerings covered hotel expenses. One man in the congregation gave twenty dollars nightly, which covered the rent for Coliseum Hall.

It was logical that Alma join forces with the Burning Bush, because they shared an identical message and a parallel history. Both groups split off from the Methodist Episcopal church and condemned it in strong language for forsaking holiness doctrine and conforming to the world's standards. In terms of theology, the leaders of both churches strongly affirmed the doctrine of sanctification and proclaimed a conservative doctrine that they equated with primitive Methodism. Likewise, their method of operation was identical; they established mission homes and conducted camp meetings, revivals, and conventions. Alma had adopted the exuberant worship style of the Burning Bush. The two groups worked together to achieve the shared goal of winning converts to Christ.

On August 5, 1902, the *Denver Post* carried the front-page headline "Prayer and Faith Alleged to Have Restored a Woman's Sight—Hundreds Give up their All under Spur of Religious Fervor." The woman referred to in the headline was Sarah Nessler, who had been blind for seven years prior to attending a Saturday afternoon healing service sponsored by the Pentecostal Union during the convention at Coliseum Hall. Cataracts on both eyes caused her blindness, and an operation has been unsuccessful in restoring her sight. Nessler testified that her daughter led her to the altar where she prayed for healing. By the time she left the altar, she recognized people she knew in the audience.

Alma's brother Charles aligned himself with the Pentecostal Union during the 1902 Denver convention. Charles stood and announced: "I will resign my pastorate at once and ally myself with this church forever. That's all the gift I can make."[17] Others in the congregation had pledged money (four thousand dollars altogether), jewelry, and property to the Pentecostal Union. Charles resigned from his pastorate at Wray, Colorado, the following day and relinquished his ministerial credentials to the Methodist Episcopal church. This act of loyalty to Alma and her organization necessitated a clean break from Methodism. He moved immediately into the missionary home at 2348 Champa Street. Charles and Alma resumed their partnership, preaching together in Sioux City, Iowa, during August and then working at a camp meeting in Buffalo Rock, Illinois.

Conventions followed in Hartford and North Grosvenordale, Connecticut, the latter location being the home town of F. M. Messenger, who had financed the New England meetings. Over the Christmas holidays, a street meeting conducted by workers in North Attleboro, Massachusetts, led to a confrontation with police when the workers refused to adjourn. One man referred to Alma as an old tramp and she responded in kind, calling him a bulldog. It turned out that the man was the new police chief (he had not yet received his uniform). News stories covering the incident resulted in crowds thronging to the services in the Samsetta Opera House to observe the "exhibitions of physical exuberance." One reporter claimed that "a description can hardly do justice to the affair. One has to go and see for himself in order to realize the extent to which enthusiasm in the guise of religion can be carried." After this statement, however, the reporter proceeded with the following account: "Men dance up and down in their chairs, wave their hands wildly in the air, scream at the top of their voices, kick their heels together and jump about the stage."[18] News of this revival reached Denver under the headline "Denver Woman Who Is Creating Sensation in East." The *Denver Times* reported that Alma was "creating a sensation by her rabid views on things religious" and causing an uproar with her "sensational utterances" and "vituperative language."[19] After Attleboro, Alma's last stop before returning to Denver was Puthnam Corner, Massachusetts, where the congregation often exceeded one thousand.

While maintaining her work in Denver, Alma spent the spring of 1903 ministering in the Colorado cities of Boulder, Colorado Springs, and Cripple Creek. E. L. Harvey, A. F. Ingler, Susan Fogg, and J. W. Lee were other evangelists in this campaign. Alma had worked with the first three in New England the prior winter. Attendance figures are incomplete, but at least one thousand attended one of the services in Boulder, and the congregation for a service at Colorado Springs numbered twenty-five thousand.

It is impossible to determine how many revivals Alma conducted independently and how many were held in cooperation with the Burning Bush between 1902 and 1905. During this time, she mentioned other services in Illinois, Iowa, California, and Texas. Although several of these engagements may have been self-supporting ventures, it appears that a majority were joint campaigns with Burning Bush leaders or other Burning Bush evangelists and workers.

LONDON REVIVAL

The fat lady came forward and preached—
preached until she was blue in the face and foaming at the mouth.
There never was a madder soul out of Bedlam.
She began pianissimo and worked herself up into a torrent
about Hell and damnation and brimstone.
—A reporter's account of Alma's preaching in London

On November 2, 1904, Alma and Kent sailed for London, England, on the SS *Baltic* to hold a revival there in cooperation with the Burning Bush. Eight people constituted the original party: Alma and Kent White, H. L. (Harry) and Beatrice Harvey of the Burning Bush, and four young women who assisted in the services before going on to India as missionaries. Services began December 1 in the Camberwell Public Baths. One of the white-tiled swimming baths had been emptied and sprinkled with sawdust, and seats had been arranged in rows on the sloping floor and a platform erected at the four-foot mark. The first night, a sparse audience of several dozen responded to posters announcing the revival with the headline "The Holy Dance Revived."

Newspaper coverage proved more effective than the posters in drawing crowds to the revival. Several articles included descriptions of the dancing on the platform. The revivalists did the two-step, the cakewalk, the waltz, and twirled like dervishes. Harry and Kent "executed an impromptu pas de deux." Alone, Harry performed "whirling jig figures."[20] The young women, dressed in blue dresses and blue bonnets with white ribbons, danced in pairs or alone, executing perpendicular jumps. Newspaper artists provided sketches of the demonstrations to accompany the articles. The free promotion of the revival in newspaper articles yielded results, and by December 3 approximately three hundred people were in the audience. The press became more sensationalistic in their sketches of the revival workers: "They howled like dervishes, danced like Red Indians, and roared out anathemas till the blood rushed to their faces and their throats became hoarse."[21] Several nights later, people quickly filled the two thousand seats while hundreds remained outside, disappointed that they would miss the "show." The unruly mob eventually rushed the gates and poured into the bath. Both Kent and Harry attempted to "quell the tumult," but their efforts proved unsuccessful.

> [Alma] stepped forward, and in a voice hoarse with emotion, harangued the hostile crowds. . . . "We are strangers and pilgrims, three thousand miles from home," she cried in tones which penetrated through the din like the notes of a trumpet. "Give us a fair hearing in the Old Country." That did it. Camberwell's patriotism was appealed to. The uproar ceased as if by magic, and the meeting, which had begun with an organized bombardment of the baths and threatened the dissolution of the dancers, ended in peace.[22]

Alma's words subdued the rowdy audience. Maybe it was this event that inspired one reporter to suggest that Alma should pose for a statue of Minerva leading the Roman Legion.[23]

The reporters' cruel caricatures of the revivalists generated intense interest. Readers learned that Kent, dubbed "Obadiah" by the press, "is rather weak in the terpsichorean line. His stiff and painful caperings resemble those of a performing bear." The source of Kent's nickname was an old song.[24] Alma fared even worse:

> Once in an ecstasy of intense excitement Mrs. Kent White rose from the pianoforte, rushed to the further end of the platform, uttering a piercing cry like an Indian war-whoop, and returned to her seat in a series of pirouetting movements of surprising rapidity. But the effect was by no means elegant. For if the truth must be told, nature has fashioned the lady upon rather a bulky model, and her caperings bore a not remote resemblance to the gamboling of an elephant.[25]

Alma did not seem to mind the harsh treatment from the press because it provided free publicity for the services. London papers referred to Alma's group as the Pillar of Fire. By this time, she had retitled her church publication the *Pillar of Fire,* and this name had become the unofficial designation of the group, just as the Burning Bush was the nickname of the Metropolitan Church Association.

Incited by descriptions in the papers, people attending the services came in a carnival mood. On December 4, the audience got out of hand and the leaders sought police protection. One paper reported the next day that "the meeting . . . had been roused to a pitch of uncontrollable merriment." One person in the crowd played a tin trumpet, with every blast resulting in laughter. The next evening, the audience "whistled and roared, and clapped and let off fireworks." Matters did not improve. When Kent and Harry attempted to preach on December 6, their words were interrupted by "deafening choruses of 'Bill Bailey' and 'For he's a jolly good fellow.'"[26]

In reaction to the disruptive crowds, a few voices called for toleration. A reporter from the *Star* interviewed Rev. Thomas Stephens, a local Congregational pastor, who "deplored the 'extravagant ridicule poured upon [the revival] by the newspapers' as tending to 'encourage a spirit of irreverence in working people.'" The *Daily Mirror* reminded its readers that the Salvation Army initially came under severe criticism and were now "admitted to be the greatest spiritual and one of the greatest philanthropic agencies of our time."[27]

Although reporters focused primarily on the physical manifestations at the revival, they did briefly ridicule the preaching: "Mrs. Kent White said that the devil—tail, and three-pronged fork, and all—was present in the bath. According [sic] with closed fists and raucous voice, she fought him for fifteen minutes ten seconds. The official result of the encounter was not announced."[28]

The revival "continued with unabated interest"[29] in London for three months. Alma's sons, John W. Hubbart, and Arthur C. Bray arrived to help on December 29. Twelve-year-old Ray played the drums while Arthur, now sixteen, assisted as pianist. Arthur Bray attempted to preach one evening, but the crowd's hissing eventually drowned him out. He was also disturbed by the British habit of talking back to the speaker.[30] Changing locations several times, the revival transferred from Camberwell Baths to People's Chapel on Wells Street for two weeks of services before moving to Lambeth Baths, where Edwin L. and Gertrude Harvey and two women missionaries from Chicago joined them.[31] The unruly audiences continued to be a problem. British police would not enter a church service unless someone was being assaulted, though workers could eject rowdy worshipers, who would be fined or imprisoned if they resisted. While this was of some help, Alma reported: "Our difficulty is that we have several hundred of them on hand at a time and the audiences become a tempestuous sea."[32] Lottie Drenk and Annie Kennedy, two of the women workers, helped keep order by expelling troublemakers.

Alma returned to Denver at the beginning of February, leaving the others to continue the revival in her absence. Kent, Arthur, and Ray remained in London and then traveled with the revival party to Wales, where a local newspaper briefly mentioned the evangelistic efforts of Arthur, who had begun preaching two years earlier.[33] Kent and the boys returned home in June.

BURNING BUSH SPLIT

The members of the undersigned committee, with great personal grief, feel compelled to publicly announce that they have thoroughly and prayerfully investigated certain recent occurrences and transactions in the life of Mrs. Kent White, of Denver, Colorado, and find that she is unworthy of our confidence and respect. Members of our committee have visited her several times and have done all in their power to bring her to repentance.
    —Burning Bush statement repudiating Alma White

What had Alma done to warrant public censure in the pages of the *Burning Bush?* The rupture resulted from an argument over a piece of property in New Jersey. Alma had accepted the title of a farm near Bound Brook from its owner Carolyn Garretson, a widow who wanted to come with several of her children to Alma's Bible school in Denver. The Burning Bush leaders contended that Mrs. Garretson had previously promised her farm to them.

The close-knit ministries of the Pentecostal Union and the Burning Bush unraveled during the fall of 1905 as both groups claimed the Garretson property.[34] Burning Bush leaders devoted a full page in their magazine for three consecutive issues in November 1905 to a denunciation of Alma. Among those who signed the announcement (quoted above) were Burning Bush leaders Duke Farson and E. L. Harvey, as well as John W. Hubbart and Arthur C. Bray, who had defected from the Pentecostal Union shortly after the controversy surfaced.

R. L. Erickson, a Burning Bush evangelist, had been holding meetings near the Garretson farm in February 1905. He stayed overnight with Mrs. Garretson, who was at this time seeking sanctification. Rev. Erickson suggested that her farm was a hindrance preventing her from the experience of sanctification. Both the Burning Bush and Pillar of Fire stressed that individuals as well as missions should operate on the "faith line," relying on God for all their needs. Many converts donated their homes and property to one of the two groups and engaged in full-time evangelistic work, earning money by selling religious literature either door to door or on street corners. The majority of the profits went to support the religious organization, although workers retained a percentage for their personal expenses. Rev. Erickson believed that Mrs. Garretson needed to relinquish her property and live by faith. He dictated a letter to D. M. Farson in which Garretson signed over her farm to Burning Bush. Alma recounted that Mrs. Garretson wrote the letter "against her own mind and will in the matter" and that God had not shown her that her property was keeping her from attaining sanctification. When Rev. Erickson left, Mrs. Garretson realized that he had taken advantage of her while she was in spiritual distress and wrote him immediately, rescinding the initial letter. According to Alma, Erickson visited Garretson's home later and "asked her if she had gone back on what she had written and she told him, 'Yes.'"[35] Carrie Garretson confirmed her mother's retraction. She was attending a meeting in West Haven, Connecticut, when Erickson approached her and said he had received a letter from her mother stating that she had changed her mind.[36] Mrs. Garretson considered the matter closed.

The Burning Bush version of the story denied that Mrs. Garretson withdrew her gift of the farm, either in writing or verbally.[37] D. M. Farson had responded to her letter (the one originally dictated by Erickson) on March 4, suggesting that if it was not advantageous to sell the farm immediately, she should execute a deed for the farm to the Burning Bush, which they would hold until it sold.[38] Erickson admitted receiving subsequent correspondence from Garretson but claimed she did not mention the farm in her second letter. Erickson acknowledged a return visit to the farm, but his version of the conversation differed from Alma's: "The last thing she said was she was going to lower the price of the farm and sell it and turn over the proceeds according to her promise."[39] This appears to be the extent of Erickson's communication with Garretson. No one in the Burning Bush accounted for the lapse of seven months during which there was no follow-up regarding the sale of the farm. This lends credence to the view that Garretson had told Erickson to cancel the agreement.

In the meantime, Alma received a letter from Carrie Garretson stating that she had read *Looking Back From Beulah*, Alma's autobiography written in 1902, and wished to attend the Bible school in Denver. Eventually, Carrie and three other members of her family, including her mother, enrolled in the Bible school. Alma mentioned the letter to

Farson and the Harveys, but, according to her, they did not refer to the property arrangement with Garretson at this time.

Alma and several workers ended up at the Garretson farm in New Jersey in October 1904. They had left Denver with the intention of holding a revival in New York City but abandoned the "Eastern Campaign," as Alma called it, because lodging in New York was too expensive. Mrs. Garretson welcomed Alma and her workers, who rented a hall in nearby Bound Brook where they conducted meetings. She told Alma about her encounters with Rev. Erickson and offered to give the land to the Pillar of Fire instead of Burning Bush. In her statement, reprinted later by the Pillar of Fire, Garretson said, "It was settled in my mind as far back as July 1st—months before the Pillar of Fire folks came to my home—that I would not give my property to the Burning Bush."[40] The Burning Bush wasted no time in pointing out this apparent inconsistency. How could she claim she had made the decision in July and also insist that she had told Erickson in early March that the deal was off?

For some reason, Alma wrote E. L. Harvey, telling him about Garretson's offer. He responded by telegram instructing Alma to come to Chicago. She refused. It is probably no coincidence that Mrs. Garretson deeded her farm to the Pillar of Fire the following day. Because Alma would not go to Chicago, the Burning Bush people came to her. First to arrive were F. M. Messenger and R. L. Erickson. Confronted with Garretson's view of her earlier meetings with him, Erickson said she was lying. Inexplicably, neither Erickson nor Alma called in Garretson at this point to clarify matters. Unable to convince Alma to renounce her claim to the farm and make restitution to the Burning Bush, the two men left, but Erickson returned three days later with E. L. and Gertrude Harvey and Duke Farson. During the ensuing stormy exchange, Farson said Alma was "full of the devil" and characterized members of her group as "liars, thieves, and criminals." John W. Hubbart, a Pillar of Fire worker who had returned from London to assist in the aborted "Eastern Campaign," attempted to defend Alma, but his efforts garnered him the label "a rattle-brained gas-bag" from Farson.[41]

As with most arguments, Alma took the opportunity to bring up another matter that disturbed her. While in London the previous winter, Henry Harvey had informed Alma that his brother, Edwin, suggested that Alma publish the *Pillar of Fire* magazine in London and the Burning Bush would take over the *Pillar of Fire* in the United

States. According to Alma, they had "laid plots to get control of the Pillar of Fire work in the United States" while she was out of the country.[42] The Burning Bush responded to this charge: "Perhaps three or four times [Alma] has told Brother Harvey that she would resign and give him their work and paper if he would take them. He refused. This has been done in the presence of witnesses, and now she says he tried to steal the Denver paper and building."[43] Given the available materials, it is impossible to determine who was telling the truth.

John W. Hubbart and Arthur C. Bray, who had returned from London with Hubbart, remained loyal to Alma until several days after the confrontation at Bound Brook. At that time, Hubbart persuaded Bray to defect to the Burning Bush. Alma stated Hubbart's motivation: "Mr. Hubbart became frightened at the thought of being cartooned and written up by these men who had so fearlessly attacked all other evangelists and religious movements."[44] Hubbart's fears were well founded. Groups such as the National Holiness Association and the Pentecostal Church of the Nazarene, individuals such as Beverly Carradine and Seth Rees, and other magazines such as *Christian Standard* and *Gospel Trumpet* had come under vicious attack in the pages of the *Burning Bush.*[45] Alma suffered from the illustrator's pen on the *Burning Bush* cover of January 18, 1906. The picture graphically portrayed the path its editors believed Alma had chosen by showing her walking in the direction of Sodom and Gomorrah. William Godbey, himself a victim of an attack in the *Burning Bush,* observed: "Perfect love is the hottest thing you will find in the world. When people profess sanctification, like some identified with the 'Burning Bush,' and yet mercilessly cartoon the Lord's people, they thus advertise their own spurious profession to the world, as perfect love speaks no ill of its neighbor."[46] Perfect love seems to have been forgotten by both groups, who now derisively referred to each other as Pillar of Smoke and Bramble Bush.

When Alma was en route from New Jersey to Denver, the Harveys boarded the train in Chicago and lured her off by pretending they wanted to seek reconciliation. Once at the Burning Bush headquarters, E. L. Harvey threatened, "It is the end of your work. We have buried every evangelist and every movement in sight and we will bury your work."[47] It was obvious to Alma that reconciliation was not on the agenda, so she left. After spending the night in a Chicago hotel, she visited a Mrs. Bowen the next day in Kewanee, Illinois, before catching an evening train to Denver. Mrs. Bowen informed Alma that she had designated one-third of the profit from the sale of a farm to the Pillar of Fire and the remaining money to go to the Burning Bush. Alma had never received her share of the money (approximately three thousand dollars). Her conversation with Mrs. Bowen provided more ammunition to hurl against her former colleagues.

The Burning Bush leadership assumed that Alma was returning to New Jersey instead of continuing to Denver. According to Charles Bridwell, "They at once rushed to Denver expecting like so many pirates to make a run on the Bible School and probably carry the majority of the students back with them to Chicago."[48] Imagine their surprise when Alma opened the door in answer to their knock. She had arrived in Denver on November 3 and, by her account, was "holding the fortresses at Denver, prepared to meet their satanic advances."[49]

The Burning Bush contingent, consisting of Farson, A. G. Garr, the Harveys, and the defectors Hubbart and Bray requested a private meeting with Charles Bridwell and Della Huffman, who were trustees of the Pillar of Fire. The two refused because they realized the purpose of the conversation was to undermine confidence in Alma's authority and win allegiance to the Burning Bush. If the Burning Bush representatives could accomplish this among the leadership of the Pillar of Fire, Charles knew it would be a simple matter "to strike a deadly blow to the whole institution."[50] Having failed to win over the Pillar of Fire hierarchy, the Burning Bush leaders next attempted to persuade students to leave the Bible school. These efforts also proved unsuccessful, so they left Denver without achieving any of their objectives.

As a result of the split between the Pillar of Fire and Burning Bush, individuals who before had worked with both groups now were forced to make a choice between them. Mary Brassfield was one worker who found herself in this awkward situation. Although she described herself as one who "belonged to the Burning Bush work in Chicago," she had been attending the Pentecostal Union Bible school in Denver for one year before the controversy erupted.[51] Mary began receiving letters from friends and relatives in Chicago urging her to abandon her work in Denver and return to Chicago. Confused by the arguments coming from both sides, she decided to pray about the matter and reported: "[God] made it very clear to me that . . . He wanted me in Denver."[52] Mary cast her lot with the Pillar of Fire despite the fact that she was converted and sanctified under the ministry of Burning Bush leaders in Chicago and had worked for the Burning Bush for one and a half years before going to Denver.

Brassfield accompanied Alma to Los Angeles during the middle of December 1905. A month later, on January 21, 1906, twenty-one Burning Bush workers in Los Angeles issued a joint statement resigning from the Burning Bush because they wished to dissociate themselves from a questionable property transaction the Burning Bush had conducted in Los Angeles.[53] Mary reported that Alma never visited the Burning Bush home or attended any of its meetings while she was in Los Angeles. Rather, prior to January 21, Burning Bush workers visited Alma individually to discuss their concerns. Two days after issuing the resignation statement, the workers moved into the Pillar of Fire missionary home in Los Angeles.[54] The February 21, 1906, cover of *Rocky Mountain Pillar of Fire* pictured a large sinking ship called the *Burning Bush* with a lifeboat, the *Los Angeles,* full of people rowing toward the shore. In case there was any doubt about the meaning, the picture was entitled "The Wreck of the Burning Bush."

B.·S. Moore and Arthur Ingler, two former Burning Bush workers in Los Angeles who signed the statement, had written Duke Farson and E. L. Harvey a letter of resignation on January 5. They listed the controversy over the Garretson farm as one reason for the letter and questioned other decisions and statements made by Farson and Harvey. They also inquired of the two men, "How could you call Mr. Hubbart a rattle-brained gas bag and be justified in putting him up to preach, and publishing his sermons and articles?"[55] It seems the attitude toward Hubbart had changed drastically with his defection to the Burning Bush.

The controversy spread to England. Apparently, Hubbart and Bray influenced their former co-workers in London to align with the Burning Bush. Eighteen Pillar of Fire workers there issued a joint statement

> sever[ing] all fellowship and connection with the said Mrs. Kent White, and the "Pillar of Fire" Church, of Denver, Colo. We are thoroughly convinced that she has been found guilty of falsifying and dishonesty. We further declare our absolute confidence in the integrity and sincerity of the editors and publishers of the *Burning Bush,* to whom we pledge our perfect allegiance and fellowship as our God-appointed leaders.[56]

Letters written by John Johnson and his daughter Sarah to Kent and Alma between August and November 1906 shed light on the Pillar of Fire/Burning Bush controversy at the international level. The Johnsons lived in Merthyr, Wales, where Kent, Arthur, Ray, and Burning Bush leaders had held services early in 1905 after the London revival. The

Johnsons wrote that Hubbart had visited their home and attempted to persuade Sarah to renounce the Pillar of Fire and join the Burning Bush. When she refused, Hubbart pointed his finger at her and told her she was going to hell. Sarah responded by calling him "a traitor of the deepest dye" and reported to the Whites that "he came like a slimy serpent to try to get us back to the meetings again." When John Johnson likewise rebuffed Hubbart's efforts to get him to align with the Burning Bush, Hubbart told him he was going to hell, too. John reported to the Whites that he had told Hubbart "his work in London and here was of the Devil and that it would come to nought."[57] Both Johnsons remained staunch loyalists of the Pillar of Fire. It has been impossible to determine exactly how many people shifted sides, in Great Britain or the United States, due to the dissension between the two groups.

Alma concluded her discussion of the controversy in *The Story of My Life* with these words: "For a number of years the Burning Bush leaders kept up the fight against me and our work, publishing nearly every conceivable falsehood that could be hatched in the regions below."[58] The Burning Bush may have continued the verbal skirmishes, but Alma won the war *and* the Garretson farm in New Jersey.

COMMUNAL LIVING AT ZAREPHATH

It was shown to me that {Zarephath} was to be a refuge for the famishing multitudes to whom would be dealt the bread of life, and where the oil of the Holy Spirit would be poured out during a spiritual famine.

—ALMA WHITE, *Story of My Life*

Severing ties with the Burning Bush necessitated a shift in Alma's ministry. Alma transferred her attention from independent revivals throughout the United States and Great Britain to developments within the Pillar of Fire. She commuted between Denver and New Jersey, supervising activities and meetings at both sites. In addition, she managed her other branches, which in the spring of 1905 were located in Colorado Springs and Cripple Creek, Colorado; Butte City, Montana; Omaha, Nebraska; and Salt Lake City, Utah.[59] Although her major focus over the next several years remained the development of the farm in New Jersey, Alma purchased property in Los Angeles (1907) and Bound Brook, New Jersey (1912). She also rented a house in Newark, New Jersey (1912) to serve as a missionary home for her workers.

Alma selected Zarephath as the name for her branch located on eighty acres of the former Garretson farm. Just thirty miles from New York City, the closest town to Zarephath was Bound Brook, New Jersey, three and a half miles away. In the biblical city of Zarephath a widow miraculously fed the prophet Elijah and her household for many days with a small amount of meal and oil (1 Kings 17). Alma intended that her members living at Zarephath would distribute the "bread of life" to those who were spiritually hungry.

Alma broke ground for the first Pillar of Fire building at Zarephath on June 11, 1906. The farmhouse on the property was too small to house all the construction workers, farmers, and those engaged in house-to-house mission work, so they stayed in tents until the additional building was completed. Alma gradually developed a self-contained city for her followers. She insisted that her church was not communal, but Zarephath's self-sufficiency undermined her disavowal. Members shared all resources and ate their meals together. Other Wesleyan/Holiness adherents also dissociated themselves from the sinful world in which they lived, but very few went so far as to actually establish communes, physically separating themselves from the world.

Alma decided on January 19, 1908, to transfer her church's headquarters from Denver to Zarephath. Alma based her decision on the fact that she was suffering from an eye inflammation she believed was a sign from God: "This affliction had been sent as a thorn in the flesh to spur me on to the right decision."[60] Once she resolved to make the change, her eye recovered. The healed eye signified to Alma that she had made the correct choice. Although Alma recorded that the group in Denver voted to go to Zarephath, one wonders how much choice they actually had.

Alma compared the relocation of her headquarters to the Old Testament story of the children of Israel leaving Egypt for the Promised Land. Zarephath symbolized Pillar of Fire's "promised land," where Alma's members would be set apart from worldly temptations. A reporter several decades later confirmed that Zarephath had fulfilled Alma's expectations: its 250 inhabitants lived "in a model community, a separate world from the one along the highway."[61]

Alma's extreme hostility toward the world reveals the extent of her sectarianism. She and her followers experienced a high degree of tension with the world around them.[62] Alma declared, in no uncertain terms, "It is unreasonable and utterly impossible to support [the world's] institutions, walk in her streets, peer in her windows, and drink of the wine cup of her fornications without being contaminated."[63] She strongly opposed her members' involvement in secular occupations and encouraged them to leave their employers when they joined the Pillar of Fire: "[God] wants people in a position to offer themselves and their services wholly to His work, and this cannot be done without breaking with the world and getting out of ungodly business entanglements."[64] When people joined the Pillar of Fire, Alma expected them to live in mission houses and give all their money to the Pillar of Fire: "There is only one way to join us. That is to turn in all your money and live with us."[65] Members received no salaries.

Alma's sectarianism shaped Pillar of Fire ministries. Although the group procured some funds from personal property donated by new members, a primary means of income was selling gospel literature door to door, in saloons, and in businesses. At this time, there were less than one thousand subscribers to *Pillar of Fire* magazine, but members distributed an additional three thousand copies of each issue. Members kept a percentage of their sales for their personal and travel expenses but turned most of the money over to the Pillar of Fire.

Alma, like most believers in holiness, eschewed fashionable clothing. For example, Phoebe Palmer had advocated "a lovely, pure, simple, and uncostly attire" in compliance with the Bible's injunction to avoid accommodation with the world.[66] The first *Discipline* of the Free Methodist church forbade fashionable clothing.[67] Alma followed the example of the Salvation Army and adopted uniforms for her members to signify nonconformity to worldly apparel. In 1907, the men's outfit consisted of loose blue knee breeches, leather leggings, high black waistcoats, celluloid collars, and Norfolk jackets; women wore blue skirts and loose blue blouses. Both men and women had "Pillar of Fire" printed on their hats: a helmet with a visor in front and back for men and a flat hat for women.[68]

Alma exerted complete control over the Pillar of Fire and its members. When a reporter asked her if the church had an archbishop, she informed him, "My word is final." The same reporter observed that Alma was "a dominating personality with no nonsense about her, she rules her people with a beneficent hand."[69] Most followers accepted Alma's style of leadership. However, one woman who had been a member for fifteen years, from 1922 to 1937, ultimately left the Pillar of Fire and authored an exposé chronicling her experience. In *My Life in a Commune*, Helen Swarth depicted Alma as a "dictator" who exacted "absolute obedience" from Pillar of Fire members.[70] She described

Alma as "a large woman with a dominant personality, ruling by the letter of the law and fear of the wrath of God and hell."[71] When Alma refused to allow her to visit a doctor, Helen went anyway and required immediate surgery. When she rejected Alma's suggestion that she marry another Pillar of Fire worker, however, there were no recriminations. Helen resented the fact that Alma and her family rated special waiters and food in the communal dining room at Zarephath. She left the Pillar of Fire when Alma informed her that she must relinquish her car to another member. Although her critique is defamatory, Helen recognized the benefits of Alma's communal system in terms of security and a sense of belonging.

Alma assumed full responsibility for her followers' well-being. Her son Arthur recounted that she cared for her converts "from the cradle to the grave."[72] She assigned church members to work at the various branch locations. Within the space of six weeks in 1907, she sent at least three letters to her branches, instructing the recipients to write a diary, to study the church tracts more, to sell two hundred papers a week, and to take a bath at least once a week.[73] Her recommendations covered a wide gamut, from the professional to the personal.

Alma's concern extended to a requirement that workers at Zarephath spend at least thirty minutes outdoors every day.[74] She never indicated the source of her conviction that fresh air and relaxation were advantageous for good health, even though other religious leaders had also emphasized health reforms. Another Wesleyan/Holiness writer, Jennie Fowler Willing, quoted Proverbs 31:17 ("She girdeth her loins with strength, and strengtheneth her arms," AV) to corroborate her position that sedentary women needed daily exercise.[75] Ellen White, a founder of the Seventh-Day Adventist church, is perhaps the most well-known advocate of health reform. In June 1863, she experienced a vision that affirmed the curative value of pure air and rest[76] and in subsequent speeches and pamphlets promoted her "heaven-sent instructions" on these and other health issues.

Alma's interest in good health likewise extended to her followers' diet. By 1914, the Pillar of Fire, like the Seventh-Day Adventist church, had adopted vegetarianism. Wesleyan/Holiness leaders such as William Godbey and Martin Wells Knapp also were vegetarians.[77] Alma bemoaned the fact that most people ate meat in spite of "every evidence that it is detrimental to their physical, moral, and spiritual welfare."[78] She attributed clogging of the kidneys, pain in the back, cancer, and rheumatic ailments to the consumption of meat. Although modern science has confirmed Alma's belief that eating meat can be detrimental to one's health, it has refined her list of physical problems. However, her conviction that eating meat has a negative impact on morals because animal flesh "feeds the flames of passion" is harder to document.[79] Alma's viewpoint was not unique, though, as both Ellen White and early nineteenth-century health advocate Sylvester Graham, of Graham cracker fame, believed meat aroused animal passions.[80] Alma's rationale for abstaining from meat also included a description of a slaughterhouse tour in Nebraska to illustrate the cruelty involved in killing animals for their meat. Following the visit, Alma reported: "I was so burdened over the cruelty I had seen that I felt I could never eat any more animal flesh."[81] Alma quoted from Genesis 1:29—"Behold, I have given you every herb bearing seed, which is upon the face of all the earth, and every tree, in the which is the fruit of a tree yielding seed; to you it shall be for meat" (AV)—to prove that God did not intend for humans to include meat in their diets.[82] Another of her reasons for advocating vegetarianism sounds remarkably contemporary. Alma observed that the tremendous amount of grain fed to cattle would be better used in making bread, which could feed hungry children around the world.[83]

Between December 1908 and February 1909, Alma discussed the issue of "sexual passions" with her followers. Members of communes are often reputed to promote sexual promiscuity or, as in the case of the Shakers, to advocate celibacy. There were a few people in the Wesleyan/Holiness movement who believed that holy living precluded sexual relations even within marriage. For example, Sarah Warner, whose husband Daniel was an early leader in the Church of God (Anderson, Indiana), became convinced that such relations were carnal or sinful.[84] Although the Pillar of Fire avoided either extreme, promiscuity or celibacy, Alma did maintain that sexual relations were appropriate only when the couple wished to conceive a child. Della Huffman elaborated in her diary on Alma's views: "She said . . . that husbands and wives were to live like brothers and sisters except when they knew God wanted them to have a child."[85] This opinion was widespread among Christians of Alma's time. It has been impossible to determine how long this viewpoint prevailed among Pillar of Fire members. As members studied relevant Bible passages "relating to the works of the flesh," Alma exhorted them to subdue "fleshly appetites and passions," which "are the most incorrigible of all depraved human instincts." Alma's concern extended to married couples who "failed to exercise self-control in their relations with one another."[86]

Between 1905 and 1909, Alma focused her attention on Zarephath, presiding over the development of a self-supporting commune and its inhabitants. She exerted a firm hand over her followers, but most did not mind the grip.

KENT EMBRACES PENTECOSTALISM
AND LEAVES ALMA

Apart from religious controversy I am your wife, and my love for you
is stronger and deeper than the day you led me to the altar,
and promised to cleave to me forever.
— ALMA WHITE, *My Heart and My Husband*

Alma visited her missionaries in Los Angeles during the first two weeks of March 1907. By this time, the pentecostal revival had been in full swing in Los Angeles for almost a year. William Seymour, an African-American Wesleyan/Holiness preacher, was the major catalyst at the Azusa Street mission in Los Angeles, which is generally regarded at the birthplace of pentecostalism. Alma had met Rev. Seymour during the spring of 1906 when he visited her Pentecostal Union Bible School in Denver on his way to Los Angeles. Her first impression was unfavorable: "He was very untidy in his appearance, wearing no collar, and had a greenish-looking brass button exposed in the band of his shirt."[87] Seymour wore no tie in accordance with the strict holiness belief that ties were unnecessary articles of worldly adornment. Despite Seymour's unkempt appearance, and his race, Alma invited him to join her and the other residents of the mission for dinner and then asked him to pray. Offering hospitality to a member of another race was highly unusual. African Americans and whites rarely sat at the same dinner table. Alma's prior cooperative revival work with African-American evangelists such as Rebecca Grant and Susan Fogg enabled her to overcome societal pressures to maintain segregation and welcome Seymour at her table. Some Wesleyan/Holiness advocates, Amanda Smith for example, credited the experience of sanctification with the ability to overcome prejudice.[88] Another author affirmed, "Holiness takes the prejudice of color out of both the white and the black."[89]

Kent attended pentecostal services and embraced pentecostalism while in Denver from October 1908 through February 1909. Prior to this time, Kent had affirmed the beliefs of Methodism that had been adopted by the Pillar of Fire. Now he began to promote speaking in tongues, which was emphasized by pentecostals. Alma worried about the affect of Kent's interest in glossolalia on her church:

> To go back now on all he had preached and taught while a minister in the Methodist Church and an instructor in our Bible School would subject us to ridicule and the charge of inconsistency which I feared we should be unable to live down for an indefinite period of time.[90]

Alma suspected Kent's promotion of glossolalia would have a negative affect on her group: "My greatest concern was for the reputation of our society on which there had never been a stain or a real cause for reproach."[91]

Kent's enthusiasm for pentecostalism renewed the strife that had periodically plagued his and Alma's marriage. It was clear to Alma that Kent now intended to follow through on his prior threats and leave her permanently: "His heart was no longer with us."[92] Strangely, Alma never mentioned the stigma of marital separation and its possible negative impact on her ministry. Doubtless, this was a serious concern, because conservative Christians, as well as society at large, frowned upon separation and divorce.

Although pentecostalism was the immediate cause of Kent's and Alma's marital discord in 1909, their marriage had weathered earlier storms. During the early years of their marriage, Alma had dealt with a contentious mother-in-law and the disillusionment of an imperfect husband as well as Kent's periodic threats to leave. Since the founding of the Pillar of Fire, Kent had often expressed dissatisfaction with his secondary role. Alma was firm in her conviction that God had called her to be its leader and that Kent was the person best qualified to supplement her labors. Although Alma portrayed herself as the sole leader of her fledgling group, some early accounts of the Pentecostal Union, however, spoke of Kent and Alma as co-leaders.[93] The discrepancy between Alma's perspective and media reports is primarily due to the fact that reporters commenting on the leadership of the Pentecostal Union stereotypically assumed Kent was the leader because he was a man. One account lends support to this explanation:

> On the center of the platform stands Kent White, the high priest and master of ceremonies, but he rarely jumps. Kent White's chief assistant and coadjutor is his wife, Mrs. Alma White. She is reported to furnish the major part of the brains and brass of the organization.[94]

If, as noted, Alma was "the brains and the brass of the organization," the reporter should have viewed Kent rather than Alma as the assistant.

Unhappy with his inferior status, Kent insisted that Alma fulfill her duties as his wife and assume a subordinate position. Alma refused to conform to this model of marriage and resisted Kent's repeated assertions of authority. She contended that "the curse of subordination is removed in a sanctified home. While the man is the recognised head, both the husband and wife enjoy equality as it was intended they should before the curse fell upon the human race."[95] Alma left little room for the doctrine of male headship in her understanding of Christian marriage. The language of equality overruled a subordinate relationship within marriage. Alma claimed to accept Kent's assertion that he was head of the home, yet her concept of "head" reduced it to a token title. She rejected outright, however, Kent's argument that, as her husband, he should lead her church. Kent chafed under Alma's dominance but initially remained aligned with the Pillar of Fire. His patience reached its limit, though, when he preached several times at a revival in late July 1909 in Brooklyn, New York, where Alma had established a missionary home. Kent was dismayed to receive only passing notice in newspaper coverage of the meetings. Acknowledgment of Alma's leadership by the press further enraged Kent, who resented the designation "Mrs. Alma White's husband" and insisted that Alma should be spoken of as "the wife of Kent White."[96] It is a challenge for any husband to accept his wife's greater prominence. Walter Palmer, the husband of Phoebe Palmer, and William Hutchinson, who was married to Anne Hutchinson, are notable exceptions.

The ultimate crisis in Alma's and Kent's marriage occurred after Kent endorsed glossolalia. He had yet to experience the gift of speaking in tongues, but his enthusiasm for the doctrine led him to encourage Alma to add glossolalia to the beliefs affirmed by the Pillar of Fire. Alma opposed the doctrine aggressively and no amount of persuasion could convince her to change her mind. Again, she rejected her husband's attempt to control her and her group. The last straw for Kent was when Alma denounced the pentecostal movement in a *Pillar of Fire* editorial. Once he came to the conclusion that God approved of "the Pentecostal baptism with the sign of tongues," Kent testified that "any word spoken against the baptism of the Holy Spirit with the manifestation of tongues caused me great pain."[97] Kent had hoped to add the Pillar of Fire to the groups that believed speaking in tongues was a valid gift of the Holy Spirit. In any battle of the wills, however, Alma usually won where her church was concerned. This instance was no exception. Kent withdrew his church membership on August 11, 1909, and left Alma two days later. After twenty-one years of marriage, Kent finally carried through on his threat to leave Alma. He headed for his mother's home in Beverly, West Virginia. Should his resolve weaken, Mother White could be counted on to reinforce his decision.

Kent's departure left Alma devastated. She labeled Kent's resignation "a Gethsemane to my soul" and recollected, "I felt as if I were walking through the valley and the shadow of death."[98] In light of the long history of marital strife, one would assume she would be relieved by his absence, but this was not the case. Despite their many quarrels and Kent's efforts to thwart her ministry, Alma clearly loved Kent. She begged him to return. Her affection is evident in a letter she wrote Kent the day after he left: "I thought perhaps you would like to hear a word from your heart-broken wife. . . . my mind goes back to more than twenty years ago, and seems to dwell there. . . . My love for you has never changed." Alma endured emotional trauma as a result of his leaving: "At times I would weep until my tears ceased to flow, but my entreaties were unheeded."[99]

Kent received a letter written September 14, 1909, by "D. H.," probably Della Huffman. She provided news of several people, but her primary purpose in writing was to inform Kent of the affect of their separation on Alma. She reported that Alma had not eaten a full meal in four weeks. Every time the fence gate clicked or the door opened, Alma hoped it was Kent returning. Concerned about Alma's welfare, Della played on Kent's sympathies hoping to influence him to come back.

Kent was unmoved by Alma's letters and Della Huffman's entreaty, and so Alma took drastic action. She traveled to West Virginia on September 21, 1909, to talk with Kent personally. It must have taken a great deal of fortitude for Alma to face her mother-in-law, who had attempted to drive a wedge between her and Kent during their early marriage. Kent refused to return to Zarephath, but he did agree to meet Alma later in Philadelphia for several days. He maintained his resistance to Alma's pleas to accompany her back to Zarephath. Likewise, she refused Kent's requests that she move to West Virginia. She returned to Zarephath immediately because, as she said, "I needed the help and prayers of my people."[100] This occasion was one of the few times she expressed her dependence on others. The church elders wrote Kent informing him that if he came back to Zarephath, he could bring several pentecostal preachers with him. This was an act of desperation. Alma seemed to have cast aside her concern over people confusing her movement with pentecostalism. At this point, she was willing to risk sacrificing her church's reputation to get Kent back. Kent arrived on October 26, not in response to the letter but because he was suffering from asthma. Alma spent the next two weeks nursing him back to health.

Alma persuaded Kent to travel with her and several followers to London to conduct a revival, leaving the states on November 13. Once in London, Kent refused to participate in the services held at Bedford Chapel, which Alma had rented. In fact, he became so antagonistic that Alma found it almost impossible to live in the same house with him. Alma established a branch in London, renting a house at 12 Glouster Road for her workers who remained there. She returned to the states on January 22, but Kent stayed in London.

It was on the trip home from London that Alma decided to write a book denouncing pentecostalism. Her attitude toward pentecostalism had acquired a personal dimension when Kent embraced glossolalia. The goal of *Demons and Tongues,* Alma's book, was "to expose this modern sorcery."[101] She attacked pentecostalism on theological and moral grounds, sparing no inflammatory language. The theological critique focused on the fact that according to the New Testament, those who had been baptized with the Holy Spirit at Pentecost spoke in actual languages; everyone could understand the message of the gospel in their native tongue. On the other hand, according to Alma, speaking in tongues represented a "counterfeit," an "abomination," and was "Satanic gibberish" because it involved unknown languages. Alma bluntly credited the devil as the originator of the pentecostal movement.[102] Challenging pentecostalism on moral grounds, Alma referred to the Azusa Street mission as a "hot-bed of free-loveism" in which "the familiarity between the sexes in the public meetings has been shocking, to say the least."[103] Needless to say, the book augmented Alma's growing reputation as a vigorously aggressive antipentecostal spokesperson.

Alma recounted her initial meeting with William Seymour in *Demons and Tongues.* She described her revulsion when Seymour prayed at her dinner table four years earlier: "I felt serpents and other slimy creatures were creeping all around me." She enlarged on her unfavorable assessment: "In my evangelistic and missionary tours I had met all kinds of religious fakirs and tramps, but I felt that he excelled them all."[104] Surely Seymour's subsequent prominent role in the pentecostal movement biased Alma's estimation of him. Her initial perception must have been more positive or she would not have entertained him in her mission home.

Although many pentecostals trace their roots to the Wesleyan/Holiness movement, holiness adherents such as Alma who rejected the doctrine of glossolalia dissociated themselves from pentecostalism.[105] Alma vehemently opposed the new movement and did all she could to denounce the "tongues heresy," as she called it.[106] Mincing no words, Alma claimed that pentecostalism "has proved to be the greatest religious farce that has ever camouflaged under the name of Christianity."[107]

Although Alma maintained her fierce opposition to pentecostalism, she still hoped to reconcile with Kent and wrote him in London during the next several months, pleading with him and sending money for his return transportation, but Kent ignored her letters and cablegrams.

Alma traveled to England in May 1910, ostensibly to find a location for a printery for her London branch. She had sent a Campbell printing press from the Denver branch to England in March. The development of the London branch paralleled Alma's work in the United States; once the branch was established, she began publishing her own literature. In this case it was the *London Pillar of Fire,* which soon began rolling off the presses. A hymn Alma wrote during the voyage to London expressed her more personal concerns: "Though loved ones have forsaken me and I am left alone / With bleeding heart help me to say, 'O Lord thy will be done.' / In agony and loneliness my heart has cried to thee / In vain the heart of those I love has turned away from me."[108] Alma had written "him" (an obvious reference to Kent) above "those" in the last line of the stanza.

Kent had remained in London since Alma's prior visit, living at the Pillar of Fire mission. Shortly after Alma's arrival in May, Kent accepted W. D. A. Hutchinson's invitation to seek the baptism of tongues at Bournemouth, England, the headquarters for Hutchinson's Apostolic Faith Church (not to be confused with the Apostolic Faith denomination headquartered in Portland, Oregon). Kent ultimately received the gift of tongues on July 7, 1910. He later testified, "God wonderfully came and baptized my soul and the word conceived in my heart was verified to me and I received the outward manifestations of the truth."[109] Kent explained his experience in detail:

> I spoke fluently for about an hour in one language, and then changed
> to another entirely different, and with the strongest kind of guttural
> sounds that worked all my vocal organs in a way that astonished me.
> That night as I went into the service I was so filled with the power of
> God that I did not know what to do. My body became so hot I put
> my hands on my flesh to see if it was physical heat, but I found it was
> not; it was the fire of God, the Pentecostal flame, burning all
> through me.[110]

Kent concluded his testimony, presented at the Stone Church in Chicago almost three years after this experience, with an oblique reference
to his separation from Alma. He admitted that separation from
"friends of the earth" was "quite a price to pay" but that "Jesus Christ
has taken their places and satisfied my heart."[111]

Alma returned to the United States without Kent in early July
1910. Kent made Bournemouth his home and urged Alma to join him
there and seek the gift of tongues, but she refused his offer. Instead, she
threw herself into the work of the church, preaching at Zarephath,
Bound Brook, and Cincinnati during July. She visited Denver in early
September and decided against closing her branch there. From Denver,
she traveled to Los Angeles where she preached and held Bible classes
for her members. While there, she attended William Seymour's mission on Azusa Street. Rev. Seymour recognized her but apparently tolerated her presence rather than asking her to leave.

Alma visited Kent in England during February 1911. He agreed to
return with her to the states on one condition—Alma was to speak in
public only with his permission. Rather than argue the point, Alma
agreed, hoping for a change of heart on Kent's part once he was back in
the states. It is surprising that Kent would trust the sincerity of her
promise. Surely he knew, based on prior experience, that she would not
abide by this restriction. Likewise, Alma was naive to assume that
Kent would change his mind; he had continually attempted to assert
his authority over her throughout their marriage. The reconciliation
was short lived. Two months after returning to Zarephath, Kent interrupted Alma when she stated that the "latter rain," referred to in the
Bible, was a promise relating to Israel rather than a reference to speaking in tongues as many pentecostals, including Kent, believed. When
Alma responded to Kent's challenge by asking the congregation to
pray with her, Kent asserted his authority physically by putting his
hands over her mouth in his attempt to silence her. Kent lost this

round. His efforts to convince Pillar of Fire members of the validity of speaking in tongues also proved futile. Kent turned his attention to pentecostal outreach in the area and, at one time, baptized forty converts in the nearby Passaic River. During the fall, he attended services throughout the Northeast under the auspices of Apostolic Faith leaders. Alma found it "humiliating" to have her group associated in people's minds with pentecostalism due to Kent's activities, but she resigned herself to the situation: "This reproach for a time we were compelled to bear."[112] It seems that she still held out hope that Kent would renounce pentecostalism and return to the fold. In the meantime, she endured the embarrassment of Kent's involvement in the pentecostal movement.

Alma and her sons, now ages twenty-three and nineteen, rented a home in Ocean Grove for the summer of 1912. Kent had returned to Zarephath on July 1 after spending more than six months with his mother in West Virginia and joined the rest of the family at the ocean resort. Alma sought to end the separation by offering to live in a home outside Zarephath. Kent rejected this concession, but during the first three weeks at Ocean Grove, there were no religious arguments.

Alma remained hopeful that reconciliation would occur: "I felt we were gaining ground and living life over again."[113] One day Kent announced that he was going to the post office but, in fact, went to Paterson, New Jersey, to assist in pentecostal services. He returned a week later but was no longer conciliatory. Within a week, he left for a pentecostal meeting in South Carolina and did not return. During the next year and a half, Kent participated in services on the East Coast and Toronto, making sporadic visits to Zarephath. In March 1913, he assumed the pastorate of Apostolic Faith's Stone Church in Chicago and pastored there for one year before making Bournemouth, England, his home. Kent and Alma remained separated from that time until his death.

BISHOP ALMA WHITE

To be the world's only woman bishop is something of a distinction.
—The Tribune

Although she was not consecrated bishop until 1918, Alma had functioned in this capacity since founding the Pillar of Fire. She maintained tight control over all aspects of her church's operation. For the next several years following her consecration, Alma continued to focus on developing the Zarephath community while supervising other branches and adding several new ones. Zarephath grew as Alma purchased eight surrounding farms between 1913 and 1918. The first improvement on the property was a power plant, which began operating in the fall of 1913. Alma supervised all details of Zarephath's development, from tree and shrub planting to the construction of a stone road between Zarephath and South Bound Brook, three miles away. In 1919, work began on an eighteen-thousand-square-foot building intended to house Pillar of Fire's publishing endeavors. Alma had secured permission to establish a post office at Zarephath in 1913, which also contributed to her goal of establishing a self-contained community.

Along with the expansion at Zarephath, Alma bought land in cities throughout the country to establish branch locations. Between 1915 and 1919, Alma secured property or houses in Plainfield, Brooklyn, Trenton, Jacksonville, Newark, Baltimore, Los Angeles, and St. Louis. Alma handled the myriad details of each real estate transaction herself, never relinquishing power of attorney. She confided that at times it took all the "physical strength and courage" she could muster to achieve the best terms possible on her property transactions.[114] Her real estate decisions were astute. Even detractors spoke admiringly of her business acumen; one compared her shrewdness to that of "a Shylock or a Rockefeller."[115]

In some cases, Alma constructed facilities such as in nearby Bound Brook, New Jersey, where Pillar of Fire built a 50-foot by 134-foot chapel (seating almost one thousand) in the fall of 1913 and in Los Angeles where the group completed a building in 1917. Although it has been impossible to determine when various branches opened or closed, Alma mentioned the following cities, besides those listed above, where her members worked between 1913 and 1920: Denver, London, Cincinnati, San Francisco, Providence, Wilkes-Barre, Pittsburgh, Omaha, and Colorado Springs.

Despite the distance involved, Alma frequently traveled to London to oversee development of her branch there and negotiate the buying and selling of property. In 1914, she purchased a building there and established the *British Sentinel* magazine. She traveled to London ten times between 1913 and 1920, making five trips during World War I. (Altogether, she made twenty-nine visits to England.)[116]

The eighth annual camp meeting at Zarephath in 1918 marked a major milestone in the development of the Pillar of Fire. William Godbey, now eighty-six, attended the meeting for the first time.[117] He had initially opposed Alma's decision to separate from the Methodist Episcopal church but had later changed his position and left the church himself. Details are sketchy, but Godbey spent several years aligned with independent Wesleyan/Holiness workers, including Martin Wells Knapp, whose separatist views had influenced Alma in 1901.[118] A reconciliation between Alma and Godbey had occurred by 1917 when Alma located a mission home near his residence in Cincinnati to make it convenient for him to dictate materials to be published by the Pillar of Fire. Godbey agreed to officiate at the Sunday service on September 1, during which he consecrated Alma bishop. It is appropriate that Godbey officiated at this noteworthy event in the life of Alma and her church because he had preached the sermon at her conversion. Alma recognized his influence at significant junctures of her religious experience by considering herself Godbey's "spiritual daughter." She expressed her admiration for Godbey: "It could truly be said that there had never been his equal as a teacher and a preacher of the Gospel since the days of St. Paul."[119]

With William Godbey's act of consecration, Alma, at age fifty-six, became the first woman bishop in the United States. The first woman to reach the rank of bishop within mainline Protestantism was Marjorie Matthews, who assumed that post in the United Methodist church in 1980. Had Alma stayed with the Methodist Episcopal church, hoping for eventual recognition of her call to preach, she would have died waiting. (The unified Methodist church, a merger of several groups including the Methodist Episcopal church, did not fully ordain women until 1956.) Instead, she took the initiative and established an independent church where she could exercise her preaching gifts unhindered by anyone else's restrictions. Like Alma, many women in the Wesleyan/Holiness movement found opportunities for leadership in urban missions at the turn of this century. In most instances, leaders consolidated these independent missions into Wesleyan/Holiness churches led by men. Alma was the only woman to found a Wesleyan/Holiness church that evolved from her missions, all the while maintaining sole control.

Also in 1918, the Pillar of Fire achieved another organizational milestone when it adopted a church discipline written by Alma's son Ray. Although the discipline was a step toward routinization, it was minimal. Power remained in the hands of Alma and her sons with

Alma assuming the position of president and Arthur serving as vice-president. The discipline established a board of bishops to oversee ecclesiastical matters while the board of trustees assumed financial and legal control.[120] Alma was clearly in charge, her two sons serving as her top assistants. In 1926, Arthur held the title of first assistant superintendent; Ray was second assistant superintendent.

Arthur and Ray assumed increased responsibility for Pillar of Fire educational institutions. They earned graduate degrees, Arthur from Columbia University and Ray from Princeton, during the 1910s in order to meet state requirements for school administrators. Arthur was dean of Zarephath Academy, which opened in 1912, offering high school classes, and also assumed the deanship of Alma White College when it was founded in 1921 at Zarephath. Alma White College offered Bachelor of Arts, Bachelor of Science, Master of Science, and Master of Arts degrees. Ray served as president of the Zarephath Bible Institute (founded in 1908 as Zarephath Bible Training School).

The Pillar of Fire purchased Westminster College in 1920 from the Presbyterian church, which had established the school, intending to make it the Princeton of the West. The Presbyterians had erected an imposing redstone building, a landmark with a panoramic view of downtown Denver, just prior to the depression of 1893. The school opened in 1907 and operated for several years before closing in 1916. Westminster College, valued at $225,000, stood empty until the Pillar of Fire bought the building and forty-five acres surrounding it for $40,000. Renamed Belleview, the school opened under the presidency of Ray, in the fall of 1920, offering a high school program. Subsequently, the Pillar of Fire established a college and seminary along with an elementary school on the Belleview campus.

Just as Alma provided an opportunity for her followers to separate themselves from employment in the world, the schools she established protected children of Pillar of Fire members from the world of public schools. Maintaining private schools became a priority for Alma, who contended that "separation is the fundamental doctrine of the Bible."[121] She developed a significant educational ministry. According to one member's assessment, the purchase of properties for educational purposes rather than the acquisition of land for church buildings best illustrates the growth of the Pillar of Fire.[122] Elementary and secondary schools at several branch locations opened over the years. Prior to 1920, Alma had started schools in Baltimore, Los Angeles (Bible training school, high school, and grammar school), and Jacksonville (grammar school). In 1921, she added a school in Cincinnati.

TRIALS AND TRIBULATIONS

I wanted no divorce, but when it was made known to me his intention was to break up our organization I felt that the time for action had come.

—ALMA WHITE, *Story of My Life*

Since her separation from Kent, Alma had persisted in seeking a reconciliation. Alma braved possible submarine attacks during World War I, traveling to England in April 1915 and again in January 1916, to talk to Kent. During the 1915 visit, Alma accepted Kent's stipulation that she refrain from preaching and singing during their time together. Kent hoped to make a home for her in his adopted country, and it appears that initially Alma seriously considered his offer. However, she ended up returning to the United States after being assured by Kent that he would soon join her there. After the visit, however, Kent wrote her: "God help me I am not going to leave the fountain of living water for any flesh or human relationships."[123] Kent decided against leaving Bournemouth, but still hoped that Alma would join him there. He wrote Alma's brother Charles and his wife Lillian in 1918 begging them: "You better try and get Alma to come and make her home with me. . . . I miss her more than words can tell."[124] After nine years of separation, Kent continued to hope for a reconciliation, but he still insisted on his terms. Likewise, Alma maintained her resolve.

By 1920, Alma suspected that the Apostolic Faith church intended to use Kent in an attempt to take over the Pillar of Fire and use it as a base of operations for expansion in the United States. Her fears intensified when Kent and leaders from his church arrived in the United States in October 1920. In December, Kent came to Zarephath in search of letters and documents to support his claim that he was joint founder of Pillar of Fire and thus entitled to half of its assets. From several statements Kent made, Alma deduced that the Apostolic Faith church intended to gain control of Pillar of Fire holdings through legal claims Kent would pursue in civil court. Alma took drastic action to forestall Kent's attempted take-over. She filed a legal complaint against Kent for desertion in order to prove that he had abandoned her and that sole leadership of the Pillar of Fire had always been in her hands. Her ultimate goal was to prove that Kent had no basis for a legal claim that he was co-founder of her church. Never one to back off from a fight, Alma took the offensive and decided to divulge the failure of her marriage in a public courtroom in a dramatic attempt to maintain control of her church. Ultimately, in her list of priorities, her church ranked higher than her marriage.

The court appearance must have been a humiliating experience for Alma. The stigma of separation, much less divorce, was a heavy burden to carry in early twentieth-century society, which looked askance at broken marriages. As leader of a conservative Christian group, Alma faced the severe judgment of fellow Christians who believed that divorce was allowable only in cases of adultery.[125] In many denominations, pastors who divorced were asked to leave the ministry. Alma never discussed this possibility in her reminiscences, but, surely, it was a matter of concern. Alma must have believed that her leadership of the Pillar of Fire would not be jeopardized by a divorce. The presiding judge dismissed the case, ruling that despite the separation, Alma and Kent continued to share a mutual affection.

Information that became available during the trial and the ensuing publicity substantiate Alma's contention that the Pillar of Fire was her church and hers alone. Alma was able to attain her ultimate objective without a divorce. She actively contributed to the media coverage of her case by granting interviews to reporters, exposing her private life to public scrutiny. She claimed, "It was [Kent's] ambition to be the head. But my people would not have him as leader. . . . It was jealousy which drove him to leave me."[126] (Although the press did not document Kent's side of the story, he later defended himself by claiming he had encouraged Alma's ministry. But he did admit he "never dreamed [she would] rise up to dominate my life."[127]) In another article entitled "Bishop Says Her Heart Is Broken," Alma informed the reporter that she was determined to endure her broken heart because "I would not give up my faith for my husband."[128] To further bolster her case, Alma authored *My Heart and My Husband* (1923), a collection of four-line stanzas narrating the story of her marital separation. Alma's strategy succeeded. The court case and the media coverage deterred the Apostolic Faith leaders from subsequent attempts to take over her church.

Without exception, Alma effectively squelched Kent's repeated attempts to limit her autonomy. She rejected his assertions of spiritual headship in doctrinal matters and in the leadership of her church. After experiencing sanctification, she pursued her call to preach in spite of Kent's intense opposition. She established her first mission and ultimately founded the Pentecostal Union over Kent's objections. Subsequently, when Kent attempted to wrest the church from her control, Alma held her ground and willingly faced the embarrassment of a public appearance in divorce court in order to keep Kent from achieving his objective. The breakup of her marriage was a high price to pay, but it assured her autonomy.

Just two years after the divorce suit, Alma again found herself in a courtroom. In this instance, T. A. Goode challenged Alma's control over her followers by suing Alma for alienation of his wife's affections due to her involvement in the Pillar of Fire. The case came to trial in February 1922. Mr. Goode accused Alma, in her words, of "exerting undue influence over people and rendering them irresponsible for their acts of charity and benevolence."[129] Goode's attorney sought unsuccessfully to obtain testimony from Alma and several Pillar of Fire members on the witness stand in an attempt to establish that Alma was a dictator who determined her followers' spiritual and material destiny.[130] The judge vindicated Alma by throwing out the case. Alma maintained firm command over her followers, but the judge's ruling denoted that her leadership was within legal limits.

The third trial that Alma faced in the 1920s was one she initiated against her brother Charles and his wife Lillian, who supervised the Denver branch in her absence. Charles had been appointed bishop in the Pillar of Fire, and Lillian served as an elder. Things did not run smoothly in Denver, and Alma made frequent trips there to resolve various conflicts.

By 1925 the situation had deteriorated to the point that Alma summoned Charles and Lillian to Zarephath for a church trial to consider, among other things, possible misallocation of church funds. Lillian remained in Denver, but Charles traveled to Zarephath to face the charges against him. Many issues emerged at the trial, held on August 27, but it appears that the primary concern was the fact that Charles appropriated Pillar of Fire money and materials for his own use. Alma feared that she would be held responsible for Charles's misuse of funds and spoke of possible prosecution due to the financial situation in Denver. Charles defended his actions, claiming that he took only enough money for his living expenses. The problem, however, was that Charles should have kept a record of all funds donated to the Pillar of

Fire and the money should have been listed on the Pillar of Fire account books before being returned to him for expenses. By an almost unanimous vote, Pillar of Fire members disfellowshipped the couple and stripped them of their ordinations. Alma left the door open for reconciliation, but Charles and Lillian never walked through it. Charles returned to Denver after the trial and assumed leadership of the People's Tabernacle, formerly pastored by Tom Uzzell.[131]

4
Expressions of Ministry in Society

KU KLUX KLAN SUPPORTERS

*The invisible Empire rose to power with the aid of ministers
from all denominations who turned their churches into
Klan sanctuaries and recruiting camps. These ministers
served the realm at all leadership levels and willingly bestowed
their benedictions upon the fiery cross.*
— ROBERT GOLDBERG *(speaking of clergy in Colorado)*

Alma claimed her first encounter with the Ku Klux Klan occurred at
her Cincinnati branch in December 1922. During an evening worship
service, two masked men in white robes entered the room and handed
her fifty dollars. A statement accompanying the money commended
Alma for promoting issues the Klan also affirmed.[1] Pastors of other
churches also received Klan contributions, often given in appreciation
of comments made from the pulpit favoring the Klan.[2] Klansmen,
wearing their robes, participated in worship services, sitting with the
congregation while clergy preached patriotic sermons and quoted
Romans 12:1, "the 'Klan verse' of the New Testament."[3]

Although Alma asserted that the incident in Cincinnati was her
first introduction to the Klan, actually she and the Ku Klux Klan had
been linked earlier that year in Denver. The March 9, 1922, *Denver
Catholic Register* printed an article entitled "Ku Klux Klan Letter." The
letter, mailed to the *Register* office, had consisted of one sentence
scrawled across the top of an issue of *Good Citizen:* "The Romanist is
the worst of all, but he and the nigger and the I.W.W., the Jew and
every other bad citizen must get out.—K.K.K."[4] The article's observa-
tion that the Pillar of Fire was "bitter anti-Catholic" probably was
based on Alma's castigation of Catholicism in *Good Citizen,* a magazine
she had established in 1913. Alma referred to *Good Citizen* as "God's
mouthpiece for exposing political Romanism in its efforts to gain the
ascendancy in the United States."[5] Alma visited the *Register* office and
informed the staff that neither she nor her followers had written the

85

threat and that she opposed the Klan. A parenthetical comment, following a listing of the article in the *Denver Catholic Register Index,* indicated Alma's later change of heart: "It was not long, however, until the Pillar of Fire was as close to the Klan as a bee is to a honey barrel."[6] Alma failed to mention this incident in her writings; neither did she indicate that initially she harbored an adverse opinion of the Klan.

The *Denver Catholic Register* provided information on Alma's anti-Catholic activities throughout Colorado in 1923 by informing its readers that she made violent attacks on priests, nuns, and the Knights of Columbus in Longmont and carried her hostile message to other northern Colorado cities as well.[7]

On the evening of May 1, 1923, Klan members visited another Pillar of Fire church, this time in Bound Brook, New Jersey, for the purpose of organizing a Klan unit among male Pillar of Fire members. Soon after the first speech commenced, a mob of about five hundred people started stoning the church from the outside while Ku Klux Klan opponents in the auditorium threw chairs. During the night, the crowd destroyed furniture, church windows, and many cars. It was 3:00 A.M. before ten state police arrived and those trapped inside the church were able to leave.[8]

Shortly after the violence at Bound Brook, the press quoted Alma: "My people are not members of the Klan, but we agree with some of the things that they stand for and we intend to assert our American rights of freedom of speech." She further affirmed, "We have no connection with the Klan."[9] By the fall of 1923, however, Pillar of Fire members no longer remained aloof from the Klan but joined it, ostensibly to acquire information regarding the Knights of Columbus, a Catholic group that was giving them trouble. Information is unavailable on the number of Alma's followers who became Klansmen, but Robert Goldberg noted that many in Colorado joined.[10] Women Pillar of Fire members became members of the Women of the Ku Klux Klan.

Alma maintained contacts with the Klan in Colorado and New Jersey. Klan leaders visited Alma when she stopped in Colorado Springs during the fall of 1923. When the Pillar of Fire building was dedicated there in 1924, the Klan sent flowers for the first service. Over the next several years, the Pillar of Fire band performed at Klan gatherings in New Jersey.

Shortly after her first encounter with the Klan, Alma began receiving invitations to speak at Klan events. She justified her decision to accept many of these engagements: "I considered it an opening to preach the Gospel, which I never failed to do in any of my messages on Americanism."[11] During 1923, Alma spoke to a crowd of 950 in Longmont and to five thousand at a Klan gathering in Princeton, Illinois, participated in a "klanvocation" in St. Louis, and appeared at a Klan gathering in New Jersey. She was a speaker at the Old Cotton Mill in Denver when Hiram Evans, national leader of the Klan, also addressed a crowd estimated at forty thousand.[12] Alma continued to lecture at Ku Klux Klan events in 1925, speaking to eight hundred in Longmont and to a large gathering in Spotwood, New Jersey.

Why did Alma join forces with the Ku Klux Klan? She discovered an ally in the Klan, an organization that shared not only her anti-Catholicism, fervent patriotism, and nativism, but also her militant opposition to modernist theology. Hiram Evans, the imperial wizard of the Klan, affirmed his group's reverence for the Bible and strongly opposed modernism, which he referred to as "atheistic intellectualism."[13] Because Alma chose to respond to the world aggressively rather than to accept the world as it was or to try to avoid the world altogether, she sought allies to assist her. Because the Ku Klux Klan promoted "old-fashioned religion,"[14] Alma recognized Klan members as fellow warriors in the fight against religious modernists.

Despite critical doctrinal differences, Alma agreed wholeheartedly with the fundamentalist critique of modernism and opposed both evolution and higher criticism of the Bible, which were primary issues in the modernist/fundamentalist controversy.[15] An article covering Pillar of Fire activities entitled "Ancestors not the Tree-hanging Kind" revealed Alma's opposition to the theory of evolution.[16] Biblical criticism had no place in the pulpit according to Alma, who asserted that it was her "business to preach the Word and not to criticize it."[17] Alma's sermons frequently attacked both biblical criticism and evolution.[18] Some Wesleyan/Holiness leaders probably shared Alma's aversion to evolution and biblical criticism, but, unlike Alma, they did not publicly align themselves with others to attack proponents of these viewpoints.

The Pillar of Fire was the only religious group to publicly endorse the Ku Klux Klan. No other Protestant denomination officially condoned the Klan or its activities. An examination of Methodist, Presbyterian, Episcopalian, Universalist, Reformed, Disciples, and Lutheran magazines by one researcher revealed a consistent opposition to the

Klan at the denominational level. Although periodicals of other denominations hedged or remained silent on the issue, "no evidence of complete and open support was found."[19]

Alma applauded the Ku Klux Klan's political successes at the height of its power in 1924: "Outstanding victories . . . were reported from Indiana, Kansas, Mississippi, Colorado, and Oklahoma. Candidates for Congress and for the governorship in these states were successful, when endorsed by the patriots."[20] The previous year, Alma had commended the Klan in New Jersey for its work in electing men who stood for law and order rather than those who wished to rescind prohibition.

Regardless of condemnation at the denominational level, some clergy in churches other than the Pillar of Fire actively supported the Klan. A survey conducted by the National Catholic Bureau of Information between 1922 and 1928 disclosed that twenty-six out of thirty-nine national Ku Klux Klan lecturers were Protestant ministers.[21] Sixteen Protestant clergy were among 102 Klan officials. Of the known denominational affiliations, Methodists, Baptists and Disciples of Christ were most highly represented.[22]

Studies of the Ku Klux Klan at the state and local levels reveal significant involvement by clergy. Colorado and New Jersey are particularly illustrative as Alma spent much of her time in these two states. The Colorado Klan in 1925 elected Baptist minister Fred Arnold to serve as grand dragon, the highest official at the state level.[23] Colorado clergy also cooperated in Klan-sponsored services, such as a prayer meeting in 1924 at the Garden of the Gods near Colorado Springs attended by three thousand people, including Alma. According to Robert Goldberg, pastors in Colorado performed a crucial function by legitimizing the Klan:

> They welcomed delegations of klansmen and eagerly accepted their donations. They gave the Klan its aura of religious respectability. The activities of clergymen in urban and rural parishes thus assumed far greater weight than the belated and ineffective resolutions of the state conventions. On the local level in Colorado, the silent observer became the silent partner.[24]

For the most part, "Protestant Denver accepted or at least tolerated the Klan and only occasionally questioned it as a legitimate response to community needs."[25] Two Denver congregations, in particular, actively corroborated with the Klan. The Grant Avenue Methodist Church and Highland Christian Church, according to Colorado Supreme Court Judge Otto Moore, "seem to have provided ardent support for the Klan. From such institutions influence radiated out in all directions; outlets were provided whereby literature and other forms of propaganda could be thoroughly disseminated."[26]

As in Colorado, individual pastors in New Jersey endorsed the Klan and actively promoted Klan activities. Methodists provided the most active clergy in spite of disapproval from their bishops.[27] Other supporters were Baptist and Disciples of Christ ministers.

Prominent religious leaders joined local clergy in endorsing the Klan. Evangelist Billy Sunday welcomed Ku Klux Klan members to his revival services.[28] When presented with a bouquet of white roses by Klan members, Aimee Semple McPherson, founder of the International Church of the Foursquare Gospel, commended the Klan: "There is work for you men to do to defend the weak and to stand as champions for those who have none to stand by them."[29]

Why the close connection between so many clergy and the Ku Klux Klan? Charles Ferguson's analysis of "Ku Kluxism" helps to explain the alliance. Ferguson considered the Klan, along with nineteen other religious cults, in *The Confusion of Tongues:*

> We made a religion of our hate. We made a God of Uncle Sam and doctrines of our national beliefs, and we found devils for our new religion among the Jews, the Catholics, and the Negroes. . . . With all this catechism and consecration we disciplined ourselves to think of ourselves as a people peculiarly ordained of God to lead humanity to the Promised Land.[30]

Clergy were not alone in condoning the Klan and actively supporting it. Estimates of national membership at the height of Klan popularity during the mid-1920s range between three and six million.[31] Who were the people who chose to affiliate with the Klan? In his revisionist study of the Klan during the 1920s, Goldberg challenges prevalent stereotypes of Klan members that associated them with their post–Civil War counterparts. Members in the 1920s lived in all sections of the country, not just the South. Very few members were vicious and cruel; neither were they "uprooted men and women suffering from psychic and societal disorders. Instead, Klan membership represented a normal individual's decision to confront real and immediate problems."[32] Sympathizers such as Alma, and pastors and laypeople of various other Protestant groups, believed the Ku Klux Klan was a legitimate outlet for addressing serious issues confronting the nation. Similarly, Kathleen Blee's research revealed that Klan members do not match the negative stereotype that subsequent generations have created. Instead, they "loved their families, acted kindly and sympa-thetically to many other people, and even held progressive views on a number of issues."[33] Alma listed occupations of Klan members: "Min-isters of the gospel, United States senators, congressmen, governors, and other federal and state officials, judges, lawyers, doctors, college professors, school teachers, bankers, manufacturers, businessmen of all classes, and clean-living level-headed men from the rank and file of our citizenry."[34] Alma's statement suggests that Klan supporters do not conform to later stereotypes.

UNITED AGAINST A COMMON ENEMY

> *Rome is the arch foe of liberty. Her system is a misfit in the*
> *United States and can never be made to harmonize*
> *with the principles of free government.*
>
> —ALMA WHITE, *Guardians of Liberty*

Alma agreed with the Klan's emphasis on law and order, morals, prohi-bition, and opposition to modernism, but the item on the Klan's agenda that received Alma's strongest endorsement was anti-Catholi-cism. Between 1925 and 1928 she published three volumes of speeches she had delivered in support of the Ku Klux Klan.[35] Of the forty-four speeches included in these volumes, two criticized Jews and one revealed Alma's racism against African Americans. The majority of the speeches were diatribes against Catholics, focusing particularly on the pope.[36] The three books contain seventy-eight illustrations, of which sixty-three incorporate anti-Catholic themes. Two of these sixty-three illustrations include Jews, identifying them with "corrupting" movies and "indecent" fashions. (One other illustration portrayed Catholics and Jews as strange bedfellows.) None of the illustrations attack Afri-can Americans. Anti-Catholicism clearly was Alma's primary motiva-tion for supporting the Klan. Several chapter titles from her books of speeches indicate Alma's concern: "Rome's Claims without Scriptural Foundation," "Shall the Pope Rule the World?" and "Rome in Control of City Governments."

Researchers have accused Alma of racism and anti-Semitism because of her connection to the Klan. For instance, although Blee lists anti-Catholicism, anti-Semitism, and racism as motivations for Alma's affil-iation with the Klan, she places more emphasis on anti-Semitism and racism. Alma explicitly attempted to disassociate herself from these components of the Klan agenda: "We had nothing against the Jews or the colored race, against whom the new order was sometimes accused of discriminating. . . . While we are opposed to the mixing of white and black blood, racial prejudice was never allowed to be fostered among our constituency."[37]

Alma threw her support behind the Klan primarily because of its anti-Catholicism but, unfortunately, accepted racist attitudes prevalent in the United States. She denounced marriage between African Americans and whites and believed in white supremacy.[38] Counteracting these ideas, though, was a willingness to associate with African Americans that, for the most part, was not evident elsewhere in society. For example, an undated picture of several women dressed in Pillar of Fire uniforms includes an African-American woman. Although the woman represented a small minority of the membership, her presence, and also Alma's evangelistic work with African Americans in her early ministry, reflect an acceptance of African Americans that was unusual during her lifetime.

Blee accuses Alma of being "violently anti-Semitic," yet her evidence consists of Alma's accusations that Jews financed the Catholic empire and controlled the motion picture industry, making immoral films, keeping theaters open on Sunday and employing Protestant women in their endeavors.[39] Although these statements are critical of activities engaged in by Jews, they do not necessarily constitute a "violently anti-Semitic" attitude.

Alma's eschatology predisposed her to look favorably on Jews.[40] One of the prophecies relating to the end times was that Jews would be restored to their homeland in Israel. Along with other premillennialists, Alma believed that a remnant would return to Israel "through whom God will work to consummate the plan of redemption in bringing about the conversion of the world."[41] Many Jews would become Christians and then evangelize the world. As a premillennialist, Alma believed that Jews would usher in the millennium.[42]

Alma's concern for the welfare of the Jews under Adolf Hitler's regime also undermines Blee's accusation. The German National Socialist Party came to power early in 1933, and, by that spring, it had initiated measures intended to eliminate the Jewish population in Germany.[43] At the Zarephath camp meeting that summer, Alma referred to the outrages Jews were experiencing in Germany.[44] In a sermon delivered a year later in Denver, Alma again deplored persecution of the Jews in Germany.[45] David Wyman has documented the almost complete silence regarding German treatment of Jews by America's Christian churches up through 1945.[46] Alma was among the few Americans in the early 1930s who spoke out against German treatment of the Jews.

Alma's anti-Catholicism, rather than racism or anti-Semitism, drew her to the Ku Klux Klan. Her antipathy to Catholics stemmed in part from her early career as a preacher. She claimed that the police who broke up her street meetings in Colorado and New Jersey were either Catholic or controlled by Catholic politicians. Alma asserted that the police who arrested her street workers on February 8, 1903, in Denver were trying to rob them of their rights as "free-born American citizens."[47] When the revitalized Ku Klux Klan emerged in the 1920s, it protested the infringement of Pillar of Fire members' right to preach on street corners, a right they believed the Constitution guaranteed them, and Alma appreciated their support: "In answer to prayer, God raised up this patriotic army in defense of our rights as American citizens."[48]

Quoting biblical references that she claimed symbolized the evils of Catholicism, Alma asserted that Catholics were pagans rather than Christians.[49] The harlot mentioned in Revelation 17 as well as the fallen Babylon in Revelation 18:2-5 represented Catholicism, according to Alma's interpretation.[50] Alma's symbolism is typical of the church-historical method of understanding the book of Revelation. This interpretive approach views Revelation as a history of the church, revealing events that are either partially fulfilled, are being fulfilled, or are yet to be fulfilled.[51] Years earlier, Alma's mentor William Godbey had called the pope the antichrist of prophecy.[52] Alma continued the tradition: the pope was "the man of sin" or "the son of perdition" described in 2 Thessalonians 2. Alma defined the pope as the "arch foe of liberty" whose aims could never "harmonize with the principles of free government."[53] She contended the nomination of Alfred E. Smith for president in 1928 was the pope's attempt to defeat prohibition and other Protestant causes. During the election campaign that year, Alma argued that if Smith won, "free speech, free press, free public schools, etc., would soon be things of the past."[54]

There had long been negative assessments of the pope in the United States, according to John Higham: "Since the Enlightenment, Americans had tended to look upon the Pope as a reactionary despot, hostile to liberty and progress alike."[55] Alma and the Ku Klux Klan did not initiate anti-Catholic sentiment but fanned the flames that had burned since the colonial period.[56]

PATRIOTISM

No one can be a true Christian without being patriotic.
—ALMA WHITE, *Radio Sermons and Lectures*

For Alma and other Klan supporters, patriotic zeal motivated their anti-Catholicism. Alma's patriotism, like her anti-Catholicism, predated the revived Ku Klux Klan of the 1920s. Proclaiming a strident nationalism, she identified patriotism as one of the Pillar of Fire church's beliefs. Referring to the establishment of Pillar of Fire headquarters at Zarephath in 1908, she wrote: "It was necessary at the beginning of our work on the Atlantic seaboard to inspire patriotism and a love of country in the hearts of the people. Patriotism was at a low ebb at this time, and I was convinced that it was as much our duty to uphold the principles on which our government was founded as to lift up the standard of true religion."[57] Alma claimed the Pillar of Fire had always stood for "100 percent Americanism,"[58] even though the term itself did not come into use until World War I. Alma regarded the Constitution as "the greatest document that was ever framed by mortal mind" and admonished American citizens to "prize the Constitution next to the Bible."[59] In retrospect, one suspects Alma's patriotism was as important to her as her theology.

According to Klan rhetoric, because Catholics owed their first allegiance to the pope, they could not simultaneously be patriotic Americans. Alma agreed and encouraged all "true Protestants and patriots" to support the Klan program, which she contended was in perfect harmony with the New Testament.[60] Of course, the Bible does not support "100 percent Americanism," but Alma's allegorical interpretation enabled her to discover prototypes of Klan members throughout the Bible. For instance, Alma likened Klansmen to biblical characters such as the three men described in the Old Testament book of Daniel, who "stood upright, refusing to bow" to a false image: "These men, the worshippers of the true and living God, feared not the edicts of a heathen king, nor to die in behalf of a righteous cause. They represent our 100-per cent Americans at this period in our national history."[61] Alma justified the Klansmen's covert activities by comparing them to

Gideon, another biblical personality, who tore down altars to false gods at night.[62]

Alma also compared the Klan favorably to the revolutionary founders of the United States. To Alma, delegates to the Stamp Act Congress in 1765 were "one-hundred-per cent Americans." Alma insisted that "the parallel between the patriots of the Revolution and those of today is obvious to anyone who has eyes to see."[63] An illustration accompanying this statement depicted patriots clad in Klan robes throwing tea overboard at the Boston Tea Party.

The Ku Klux Klan propagated a militant Protestantism to defend America's traditions and ideals, which it felt were threatened by the large number of immigrants, many of whom were Catholic. Between 1891 and 1920, 18,218,761 immigrants arrived in the United States.[64] The Ku Klux Klan appealed to fears, frustrations, and hate, which it then focused on these immigrants who served as scapegoats for the problems faced by the United States, particularly in the burgeoning cities where most immigrants settled.

Increased immigration fueled widespread fears that Rome's goal was to take over America. Samuel F. B. Morse, inventor of the telegraph, conceived the papal plot theory, which purported that the Catholic hierarchy in Rome intended to overthrow democracy in the United States by encouraging Catholic immigration.[65] Despite its dubious history, Alma kept the rumors of a papal plot alive in the pages of *Good Citizen.*

Arthur White, Alma's son, attributed the Klan's popularity to the belief that its members would prevent a Catholic take-over of the country:

> If there are students of history today who are puzzled over the rise of the "invisible Empire," they could better understand it in learning, as Mother, from firsthand experience can tell them, of an era of militant, aggressive open determination of that power we know as "Rome" to convert our democracy into a religio-political autocracy. It turned loose rivers of propaganda, and like a great flood tide the menace would have covered all the land, had not the dikes of patriotism been thrown up to direct it to the great gulf of oblivion.[66]

Alma, too, credited the Klan with preventing "the hordes from the Old World" from uniting church and state and forcing all Americans to become Catholic.[67] Alma's nativism, like the Klan's, stemmed from anti-Catholic roots.

The fact that immigrants were slow to adjust to American culture worried Alma because "it is impossible for people to enlist their best energies in a common cause unless their nationality, habits, customs, and even their religion in the broader sense, are much the same."[68] Most Americans worried about the immigrants' resistance to assimilation. Even Charlotte Perkins Gilman, a prominent feminist theoretician who had earlier worked with Jane Addams, reverted to the opinion then prevalent in society:

> But let us, before it is too late, for the sake of those splendid visions of the past, and our own more splendid visions of the future, protect ourselves from such a stream of non-assimilable stuff as shall dilute and drown out the current of our life and leave this country to be occupied by groups of different stock and traditions, drawing apart, preserving their own nationality, and making of our great land merely another Europe.[69]

Suffragists had appealed to fears aroused by the arrival of millions of immigrants by the turn of the century with the reasoning that the votes of native women would counteract those of immigrant men, thus assuring the preservation of American values. Their plea for suffrage, originally based on natural rights, degenerated into an expediency argument that women's vote would outnumber the foreign-born vote.[70]

Alma argued that due to immigration, "moral standards have been lowered and crime stalks abroad in the land."[71] For these reasons, and because of her fear that immigrants would destroy "civil liberties and rights guaranteed by the Constitution," Alma advocated restrictive immigration as did the Klan.[72] Along with many other Americans, Alma was frightened by the large number of immigrants from Southern and Eastern Europe. She favored quotas limiting immigrants from these areas because most of them were Catholic.[73]

Alma's anti-immigrant views were typical of her day. Many Americans were quick to point out the differences between the "new" immigrants from Southern and Eastern Europe, who began coming in increasing numbers after 1880, and the "old" immigrants, who had come earlier.[74] Although Alma objected to the new immigrants because of their Catholicism, New England intellectuals who founded the Immigration Restriction League in 1894 developed the case that restriction was necessary to maintain racial purity. Members of the Immigration Restriction League feared racial purity would be lost when immigrants intermarried with Americans.[75] Restrictionists ultimately succeeded in passing the Johnson-Reed Act of 1924, which superseded a provisional law adopted in 1921. The Johnson-Reed Act established immigration quotas based on the 1890 census, which resulted in severely limiting the number of immigrants from Southern and Eastern Europe. Overall, immigration was limited to 150,000 a year with a maximum of 5,000 immigrants from Italy.[76]

CATHOLICS, THE KLAN, AND WOMEN

> *{Rome} hates any movement that tends to the uplifting*
> *and enlightenment of the female sex. When Christ came,*
> *He placed woman by the side of her husband and sons,*
> *but Rome has never ceased to make a protest,*
> *and is therefore opposed to equal rights for the two sexes.*
> —ALMA WHITE, *The Guardians of Liberty*

Another source of Alma's anti-Catholicism was her belief that the Catholic hierarchy was a major obstacle in the attainment of woman's suffrage. Other than a few notable exceptions, most Catholic journals, newsletters, and clerics opposed suffrage for women.[77] The cover of the January 1919 *Good Citizen* portrayed Catholic opposition toward suffrage, depicting "Columbia" playing the tune "Votes for Women" while Uncle Sam looks on and a dog with "Rome" written across his back howls. Addressing the dog, Uncle Sam asks, "What's the matter Towser, don't you like that tune?"[78] Alma contended that Catholic opposition to woman's suffrage reflected an antagonism against granting any rights to women. Echoing his mother's position, Arthur White identified Catholicism as women's enemy: "One of the greatest factors contributing to the strength of the chains which enslave thousands of modern women is a false doctrine of the Roman Catholic Church."[79]

Alma traced the Catholic church's opposition to women's rights to the pope, whom she accused of attempting to thwart any progress in women's status. Her position suggests the veracity of Higham's generalization:

> The new religious xenophobia in the years after 1910, while building on the historic identification of popery with tyranny, went significantly further. It frequently displaced a subdued but unmistakably progressive response to social problems, its principal spokesmen hinted that the Pope stood in the way of all social improvement.[80]

Alma perceived that the pope obstructed social improvement by opposing women's rights. In Alma's estimation, opponents of suffrage and other rights for women were enemies of progress.[81]

Because the Ku Klux Klan was an ally in the fight against Catholicism, Alma assumed its opposition to Catholics also generated from concerns relating to women's rights: "We are looking to the Knights of the Ku Klux Klan to champion the cause of woman and to protect her rights."[82] The Klan creed included the statement: "I believe in the protection of our pure womanhood."[83] Whereas Alma's broader understanding of protection depended on increased rights for women, the Klan had a different agenda in mind.

At first glance, it appears that Alma looked to the wrong group to join her in the quest for women's rights. There is, however, some evidence supporting Alma's perception that the Klan was an advocate of women's rights. One source for this conviction was the Klan's emphasis on law and order. This focus benefited women because, according to Alma, "women have always been the greater sufferers under the violation of law; and those who stand for law-enforcement are the espousers of woman's cause."[84] Alma assumed that the Klan promoted law enforcement as a result of its commitment to women's rights. Alma also believed the Klan's advocacy of temperance reflected an awareness of women's suffering due to the ravages of alcohol. The Klan itself did not appear to recognize the correlation between these two issues and women's rights.

Pro-women elements of the Klan did exist, however. Colorado Governor Morley, elected by the Republican/Ku Klux Klan landslide in 1924, ordered Klan members in the Colorado legislature to support a minimum-wage bill for women. During the same session, Klanswomen in the Colorado House of Representatives sponsored legislation permitting women jurors in Colorado courts and promoting the dissemination of birth control information and the manufacture and sale of contraceptives.[85] The birth-control bill was a radical measure even among women's rights advocates. Some women reformers and physicians, most notably Frances Willard and Elizabeth Blackwell, favored the passage of the Comstock Act of 1873, which forbade the distribution of contraceptives or information regarding contraceptives. Prominent suffragists such as Carey Chapman Catt and Jane Addams refused to support Margaret Sanger's crusade to legalize the dissemination of birth-control information.[86] Alma advocated the most popular means of limiting one's family which was by sexual abstinence or "voluntary motherhood."[87] Thus, while Alma supported the selection of women as jurors, she probably did not join with Colorado Klanswomen in promoting contraceptives.

Blee's study of women Klan members provides further evidence for Klan support of women's issues. *The Fiery Cross,* a Klan periodical, "reported favorably" on National Woman's Party efforts to elect women to Congress. The Klan's *Fellowship Forum* included a page entitled "The American Woman," which included information on women's rights efforts, and Lulu Markwell, who served as head of the national Women of the Ku Klux Klan in 1923, had actively worked for passage of the women's suffrage amendment.[88]

Although these examples of Klan advocacy of women's issues challenge the stereotype of the Klan, Goldberg correctly cautions: "The list is too small and overshadowed to significantly cleanse the organization's traditional reputation."[89] It is likely that Alma was aware of the legislation expanding women's rights in Colorado, but such action represents the exception rather than the rule of Klan priorities. Alma justified her anti-Catholicism by pointing to the Catholic church's opposition to women's rights. She assumed, incorrectly, that the same concerns contributed to the Klan's hostility toward Catholics.

Alma's association with the Ku Klux Klan was an unholy alliance. In light of their mutual concerns, the coalition is understandable, though regrettable. Both opposed modernist theology. They shared a zealous patriotism and a fervent nativism that excluded Catholics from their narrow interpretation of 100 percent Americanism. Alma believed the Klan was God's instrument for eliminating the "Catholic threat."

THE RELIGIOUS BASIS OF FEMINISM

*There is nothing more unscriptural and more opposed
to the principles of the New Testament than discrimination
between the sexes in both Church and State.*

—ALMA WHITE, *Story of My Life*

Alma confronted the ideology of woman's sphere when she initiated her preaching career. Clergy had promoted the notion of woman's sphere when they admonished Alma during her early ministry to maintain her place in the home rather than preach in the surrounding neighborhoods. Predictably, Alma rejected attempts to confine a woman's place to the home. She agreed with Sarah Grimké, who had defended her right to publicly denounce slavery when she was challenged in 1837: "Our views about the duties of men and the duties of women, the sphere of man and the sphere of woman, are mere arbitrary opinions, differing in different ages and countries, and dependent solely on the will and judgment of erring mortals."[90]

Subsequently, suffragists bluntly challenged the origins of woman's sphere, attributing the idea to custom and misinterpretation of the Bible.[91] One suffragist maintained that men, whom she called "God's self-ordained proxies," had sought to limit women's options.[92] Alma, likewise, insisted that the doctrine of woman's sphere originated not with God but with men. God had initially intended woman's place to be beside man as his social and mental equal.[93]

Alma was not fooled by the rhetoric employed to convince women of the benefits of woman's sphere: "[Men] will try to satisfy her with toys and flattery, telling her that she is to be the queen of the home where she will be able to wield a more powerful influence, when the fact is, she often occupies the position of a servant and a very menial one at that."[94] Unsatisfied with the "powerful influence" exercised by the "queen of the home," Alma redefined woman's sphere, broadening its parameters to encompass the world and renouncing any boundaries imposed on women by the doctrine. Alma's definition of woman's "proper sphere" and "intended sphere" bore no relation to the limiting dictates that sought to confine women to the home.[95]

The Wesleyan/Holiness movement developed a biblical hermeneutic that supported women's activities beyond the boundaries of woman's sphere. Holiness believers sought to emulate the primitive church of the New Testament era, which "placed woman side by side with man as a teacher, worker and administrator."[96] Holiness adherents documented the role of women in primitive Christianity and sought to restore to women the place they had initially filled. As a result of this emphasis, women played an important part in the Wesleyan/Holiness movement from its inception. In an effort to pattern themselves after the primitive church, Wesleyan/Holiness groups such as the Pillar of Fire affirmed women's right to preach and assume leadership positions. Although the argument was initially intended to justify women's occupation of the pulpit, Alma and others extended it to incorporate women's involvement in other areas of society as well.

Phoebe Palmer's preeminent place in the founding of the Wesleyan/ Holiness movement has been noted. Her theology and her life illustrate the feminism implicit in holiness doctrine.[97] Her reformulation of Wesley's doctrine of holiness, previously outlined, contained feminist implications. Seekers put their all on the altar and claimed the experience by faith rather than passively waiting for God to act. The

Holy Spirit worked directly with them in accomplishing the work of holiness. As interpreted by Palmer, the doctrine of holiness offered autonomy to women in that they sought the experience as individuals in their own behalf. They played an active part in seeking the second blessing by placing everything on the altar of Christ. Palmer's insistence on public testimony following the experience of holiness also fostered feminism in terms of autonomy. Empowered by the Holy Spirit, women spoke in public rather than risk losing the experience of sanctification.[98] To do so directly challenged prevalent attitudes and customs that had hindered their autonomy. Palmer's emphasis on public testimony compelled women to surmount the invisible barriers of woman's sphere, which sought to circumscribe their actions outside the home.

Palmer did not identify herself with the woman's rights movement, but her religious activities stretched the limits of woman's sphere. Along with providing the theological rationale for women's increased role in religion, Palmer served as a role model for other women, the most notable example being Catherine Booth. Palmer's ministry, as well as her theology, expanded the concept of woman's sphere so that it included women's public involvement in the church through testifying and preaching. Like most of the suffragists, Palmer did not directly challenge the doctrine of woman's sphere but extended it by redefinition.

Biblical texts that Wesleyan/Holiness leaders appropriated to affirm women's right to preach also supported women's equality beyond the pulpit. Although their hermeneutics generally was limited to the discussion of women's right to preach, there were notable exceptions. B. T. Roberts, founder of the Free Methodist church, and Jennie Fowler Willing, a Methodist lay leader, are among Wesleyan/Holiness believers who used the Scriptures to bolster their conviction that Christianity supported equality for women in the pulpit as well as in all other areas of life. One chapter of Roberts's *Ordaining Women* contained examples of legal discrimination against married women.[99] Willing referred to the Bible as women's "one book of emancipation and privilege."[100] Because Alma never mentioned her indebtedness to anyone for her biblical views on equality, it is difficult to trace the source of her hermeneutic. She had conducted revivals jointly with Free Methodists, so she may have been familiar with Roberts's *Ordaining Women*, and she reported reading *Guide to Holiness* in 1897, during which time Jennie Fowler Willing contributed a monthly column.[101] Alternatively, Alma could have developed her perspective independently and then had it confirmed as she encountered the work of others.

Early proponents of women's rights likewise had used the Bible in their arguments for suffrage and women's increased activity in society. Due to the Protestant hegemony in American culture during the nineteenth century, the Bible occupied an important place in public debates on any issue. Therefore, it was crucial for advocates of women's rights to provide the biblical basis for equality. Sarah Grimké's *Letters on the Equality of the Sexes and the Condition of Women* (1838) addressed a full spectrum of women's rights issues. She based her case on the Bible because "most every thing that has been written on this subject, has been the result of a misconception of the simple truths revealed in the Scriptures, in consequence of the false translation of many passage of Holy Writ."[102] Elizabeth Wilson authored a comprehensive biblical basis for women's equality in *A Scriptural View of Woman's Rights and Duties.* Suffragists consulted her 376-page defense of women's rights for ammunition from the Bible to promote their arguments.[103] Throughout the seventy-two-year campaign for women's right to vote, suffragists resorted to the Bible to sustain their arguments. Elizabeth Cady Stanton voiced the position of many suffragists when she claimed that "the Gospel, rightly understood, pointed to a oneness of equality."[104]

Pillar of Fire members followed Alma's lead and expounded a feminist hermeneutic. L. S. Lawrence, a charter member of the group and the undisputed theologian of the movement, asked, "But where in the Bible do we find that a woman should be denied the privilege of doing the work God has called her to do, simply because she is a woman?" He further contended, "To deny [woman] the same rights and privileges as man enjoys is not in accordance with the teachings of the Bible."[105]

Lee Anna Starr, an ordained Methodist Protestant pastor and suffragist, authored *The Bible Status of Woman* in 1926.[106] Although not contributing to the initial formulation of Alma's hermeneutic, it corroborated her perspective. A review of Starr's book by Arthur White merited three articles. Arthur summarized the book's topics, which included Genesis 3:16, women under the Mosaic dispensation, Jesus' attitude toward women, and the relevant writings of Peter and Paul. Using the adjectives "remarkable," "splendid," and "monumental," Arthur richly praised Starr's work and repeated his accolades in later articles.[107]

Not everyone agreed with Alma and other feminist apologists that the Bible advocated women's equality. Opponents of equality also appealed to the Bible to support their position. Alma and others attributed the opposing viewpoint to mistranslation and misinterpretation.

Firmly convinced that equality was God's will, Alma vigorously promoted women's equality and rested her case on Scripture. The feminist hermeneutic formulated by Alma, by other Wesleyan/Holiness adherents, and by suffragists corresponded considerably. A resolution adopted at a suffrage convention in Connecticut in 1869 offers a shorthand version of feminist hermeneutics, touching on three common themes:

> Resolved, That this equality of position and rights we believe to have been intended by the creator as the ultimate perfection of the social state, when he said, "let us make man in our image, after our likeness, and let THEM have dominion"; and to have been a part of our Savior's plan for a perfect Christian society, in which an Apostle says, "there is neither bond nor free, there is neither male nor female."[108]

Alma's biblical declaration of equality incorporated identical themes: the creation story in Genesis, the example and teachings of Jesus, and the scriptural passage quoted from Galatians 3:28.

Alma believed that God's plan for equality of the sexes commenced with creation. She and other feminist interpreters stressed that Genesis 1:27–28 announced the equality of the first man and woman because God created both in God's own image, blessed them both, and gave them dominion over all living creatures:

> So God created humankind in his image, in the image of God he created them; male and female he created them. God blessed them, and God said to them, "Be fruitful and multiply, and fill the earth and subdue it; and have dominion over the fish of the sea and over the birds of the air and over every living thing that moves upon the earth."

Alma frequently preached that God granted man and woman equal dominion over God's creation in the beginning because God made no distinction between the sexes.[109] Equality was not simply descriptive of an idyllic past that was never to be recovered but was a present goal. Alma affirmed: "There is but little hope for the human race until woman takes the place accorded her by the Creator, as shown in Gen. 1:28."[110] Articles by Pillar of Fire members reflected Alma's hermeneutic. Grant Cross, a Pillar of Fire minister and trustee, elaborated on this passage: "In Genesis 1:27–28 we learn that God created man, both male and female, in His own image, and gave them joint dominion over all the earth. Thus we see that God's plan concerning the man and the woman was that they should stand on an equality as regards all affairs of life. 'Let *them* have dominion . . . over all the earth,' was the divine decree."[111]

The affirmation of equality merited inclusion in the Pillar of Fire *Catechism:*

> What was the best of all God's creation? Man and woman, who were to have dominion, or rule, over all living creatures. "Be fruitful, and multiply, and replenish the earth, and subdue it; and have dominion over the fish of the sea, and over the fowl of the air, and over every living thing that moveth upon the earth."[112]

Those opposing equality used the creation account in Genesis 2 to demonstrate their belief in God's endorsement of women's subordination. Creation of man and woman occurs simultaneously in Genesis 1:27, whereas woman is created after man in Genesis 2:21–22: "So the Lord God caused a deep sleep to fall upon the man, and he slept; then he took one of his ribs and closed up its place with flesh. And the rib that the Lord God had taken from the man he made into a woman and brought her to the man." Opponents of women's equality claimed the precedence of man in creation in this account signified the subordination of woman.[113]

Naturally, Wesleyan/Holiness advocates of women's equality challenged this interpretation and reversed the argument, contending that because woman was a refinement of man, she was superior to him. They also amplified the meaning of "helpmeet" found in Genesis 2:18, where God refers to woman as a helpmeet who will assuage the man's loneliness. B. T. Roberts quoted Adam Clarke's *Commentary* to illustrate that "helpmeet" did not mean servant or indicate inferiority of status as generally assumed, but rather it signified a companion who was equal: "*I will make him a help meet for him; ezer henegedo,* a help, a counterpart of himself, one formed from him, and a perfect resemblance of his person. If the word be rendered scrupulously literally, it signifies one *like,* or *as himself,* standing *opposite to* or *before him.*" Agreeing that helpmeet signified equality, Grant Cross argued that woman "was to participate equally in the social activities of life as well as to share its obligations."[114]

Another text used by those opposed to equality between the sexes was Genesis 3:16b, "Yet your desire shall be for your husband, and he shall rule over you."[115] Feminist interpreters countered the contention that God sanctioned female submission by insisting that this verse was prophetic rather than the command of God condoning patriarchy.[116] The verse prophesied that the husband would rule the wife as a result of the fall rather than because God intended male domination. The prophecy of Genesis 3:16b came to pass due to man's superior physical strength and could not be attributed to divine decree. Alma and B. T. Roberts were among those who shared the opinion that male physical strength accounted for the oppression of women.[117] Grant Cross forcefully stated the case that Genesis 3:16b was prophetic:

> But now as both had fallen from their original perfection and inwardly partaken of the Satanic nature, what could follow in the future of unredeemed human existence but oppression and injustice on every hand—a perverted state of society. Under such evil circumstances and influences the strong invariably take advantage of the weak and assume the supremacy; and God who clearly foresees all coming events revealed to the woman her future lot saying, "He shall rule over thee." Not that it was His plan or that He predestined the woman to such a fate; it was a revelation to her of the inevitable results of the fall. They both had turned aside from the right course, and so would have to reap the results of their digression. Considering the subject from this point of view, we hold that the words, "He shall rule over thee," were uttered in the spirit of revelation or prophecy, rather than that of an edict giving the man such authority.[118]

The example and mission of Jesus provided a second biblical source for Alma's conviction that equality was God's design. Jesus came to overthrow the subordinate status of women that had prevailed since the fall. Alma's analysis reflects the viewpoint of Christian feminists: "But Christ, the seed of the woman, was promised, who would bruise the serpent's head and restore her to the place accorded her by the Creator as the helper and co-administrator with man."[119] Jesus' coming signified the restoration of equality between men and women that was present at creation.

Jesus' words and actions reflected his commitment to equality. L. S. Lawrence pronounced, "In a study of the New Testament you will readily see that he recognized the woman as being the equal of man in every sense of the word." Arthur White agreed: "It is perfectly clear that His treatment of women was revolutionary; it ushered in a new day; it represented an astounding social reform."[120]

Alma, along with Jennie Fowler Willing and others who viewed Jesus' relation to women in a positive light, called Jesus "the great emancipator of the female sex."[121] Jesus' mission of emancipation was not restricted to his earthly ministry. Alma stressed that until women's emancipation was attained, "the clanking of the chains of women will still be heard in the mind of a merciful Redeemer."[122] Pillar of Fire member Carolyn Staats urged women readers to draw freedom from the risen Christ, who was one of the greatest sources of freedom.[123] Alma claimed Christ's liberating work was evident in the present and would continue until liberation was fully actualized at the millennium, when Christ returned to establish a reign.[124]

Galatians 3:28 was the third biblical source nourishing Alma's emphasis on God-given equality: "There is no longer Jew or Greek, there is no longer slave or free, there is no longer male and female; for all of you are one in Christ Jesus." Opponents of women's rights maintained that male and female are one only in God's spiritual domain and that the message of this verse does not apply to women's rights in church or state. This understanding limited the declaration of Galatians 3:28 to spiritual matters; salvation is equally available to men and women. As already indicated, the Wesleyan/Holiness hermeneutic adopted by Alma incorporated this verse in its defense of women's right to preach. Alma, glimpsing the liberating vision of the verse in the state as well as the church, countered its restrictive application, as did B. T. Roberts, who proposed: "We must give this verse its full, natural, comprehensive, broad meaning. We must understand it to teach, as it actually does, the perfect equality of all, under the Gospel, in *rights* and *privileges,* without respect to *nationality,* or condition, or sex."[125] Gilbert Haven, a prominent Methodist Episcopal bishop, referred to Galatians 3:28 as Paul's "great doctrine of 'Woman's Rights.'"[126] Alma shared the conviction that this verse endorsed a broad platform of rights for women.

Although the doctrine of holiness fostered autonomy in women in several ways, the biblical hermeneutic adopted by Alma further fostered women's autonomy and quest for equality. Incorporating themes from Genesis, the example and mission of Jesus, and Galatians 3:28, Alma argued for an equality that would encompass the full range of women's rights.

ALMA WHITE AND THE NATIONAL WOMAN'S PARTY

> *I gave a message on Woman's Chains, taking some statements
> from the National Woman's Party magazines and also
> from my own writings on the subject.*
>
> —*Alma White*

Ideologically, Alma and the National Woman's Party were in the same camp: they shared the conviction that women were equal to men. Alma's understanding of equality was biblically based, whereas in contrast, the National Woman's Party relied on the natural-rights argument developed by the early suffragists.[127] Even though her basis for equality differed, Alma supported the NWP's commitment to equality and agreed with it in six significant ways. These areas of unanimity include the use of aggressive tactics, the demand for suffrage, the recognition that the battle for women's equality did not end with the passage of the suffrage amendment, the insistence that women use their vote, advocacy of women's increased role in government, and support of the Equal Rights Amendment.

Alice Paul and Harriot Stanton Blatch, two leaders of the National Woman's Party, had worked with the suffragettes in England and imported their aggressive methods to the United States. Because Alma employed the same tactics in her ministry, she was not offended by public demonstrations such as street meetings and parades, which suffragettes organized to publicize their cause. Alma admired the British suffragettes' commitment, having observed their work during her trips to England before World War I:

> The women of England were being arrested, imprisoned, and forcibly fed in their contention for the ballot. They had shed no blood, but had to suffer indignities from officers who were continually on their track. They were thrown into prison with common criminals, where they showed a willingness to die, if necessary, for human rights.[128]

Given Alma's own style of forcefully pursuing her right to preach, it is understandable that she approved the suffragettes' efforts to attain political rights by active means. On the other hand, members of the National American Woman Suffrage Association disclaimed the term *suffragette* and sought to win converts through education. They preferred to be called *suffragists* in an effort to dissociate themselves from the National Woman's Party and its methods. Although the National Woman's Party did not resort to rock throwing and other violent actions undertaken by the British suffragettes, it sponsored nonviolent media events designed to embarrass President Wilson and call attention to the fact that he was not fulfilling his campaign promise to work for suffrage. During the two-year period beginning June 1917, police arrested more than 500 National Woman's Party members and 166 received jail sentences of up to seven months, often on charges of obstructing sidewalk traffic. They picketed the White House and burned Wilson's speeches on the sidewalk in front of the White House because his democratic rhetoric did not apply to women without the vote in the United States. Alma likely commended the National Woman's Party's adoption of the suffragettes' strategies in the United States during the final years before suffrage for women was adopted.

Women's equality and the demand for suffrage were constant themes in Alma's sermons and Pillar of Fire literature before and after World War I. It has been impossible to determine when Alma first identified herself as a suffragist. A 1916 newspaper article quoted Alma's son Ray, who claimed the Pillar of Fire had supported suffrage from its inception in 1901. The article quoted Ray's conviction that "not until the women vote will this be a truly free nation."[129] The Pillar of Fire periodical *Good Citizen* endorsed suffrage. Alma's other son, Arthur, wrote "Let The Women Have the Vote" in the December 1918 issue, and Pillar of Fire member Ida C. Turner advocated suffrage in an article a year later.[130] During 1918 and 1919, *Good Citizen* reprinted articles from *Christian Herald, Pathfinder,* and *Public Ledger* favoring suffrage for women. Information reprinted in the "News Items" department of *Good Citizen* documented the final drive for suffrage.[131]

Other Wesleyan/Holiness preachers and groups shared Alma's support of woman's suffrage. The Wesleyan Methodist church (now the Wesleyan church), the first denomination to include a statement affirming holiness in its creed, had hosted the first woman's rights meeting at its church in Seneca Falls, New York, in 1848. Gilbert Haven served as president of the American Woman Suffrage Association. Hannah Whitall Smith, author of the best-selling *Christian's Secret of a Happy Life,* and her husband Robert were "important allies of the woman suffrage movement."[132] The *Christian Herald,* a Wesleyan/Holiness periodical, devoted eight articles to suffrage between 1910 and 1920.[133] An editorial in 1916 contended that the case for suffrage was "founded on reasonableness and justice," and a subsequent article urged readers to support the suffrage amendment.[134]

Alma applauded the passage of the suffrage amendment when

Tennessee became the thirty-sixth state to ratify it on August 18, 1920. In her words, the victory of suffrage was one of the "crowning events in our national history," representing "the triumph of the Cross in the liberation of women who in their inequality with the opposite sex had worn the chains of oppression."[135]

The majority of suffragists and most Americans believed that passage of the woman suffrage amendment signified that the battle for women's rights was won, and they questioned the need for continued agitation. Alice Paul, leader of the National Woman's Party, opposed this viewpoint and stated her position bluntly: "It is incredible to me that any woman should consider the fight for full equality won. It has just begun."[136] Alma agreed wholeheartedly with Alice Paul and declared in a sermon that "the world continues its opposition to [woman's] liberation in social, civic, and religious circles, determined to perpetuate her chains."[137] Alma preached on "Woman's Triumph" in winning the ballot but stressed that suffrage did not end women's subordination: "And even though [women] may be legally entitled to the ballot it may take years to free them from the bondage of subordination to their political masters, many of whom will, no doubt, continue to try to humiliate and intimidate them in the exercise of their God-given rights."[138] The National Woman's Party and Alma White formed a marginal minority who realized that suffrage was only one step toward equality.

In the early 1920s Alma frequently preached the sermon titled "Inequality of the Sexes in Church and State."[139] In her commencement address at Zarephath in 1922, Alma called for "a reconstruction of society in this age on the basis of women's equality,"[140] and during commencement exercises the following year, Alma declared that "religious and political equality for the sexes" was a part of the Pillar of Fire creed. Alma denounced inequality in Colorado Springs earlier in 1923 and also at the Zarephath camp meeting that summer.[141]

Like the National Woman's Party, Alma urged women to vote: the suffrage amendment "opened the door of opportunity for women," but they could only cross the threshold by voting.[142] Alma did not naively believe that men would automatically recognize women's equality. Women must work to change their status by demanding their rights at the ballot box: "It is the exception rather than the rule for men to favor a larger political and religious sphere for women's work, and not much help or encouragement can be expected from them. The women then would as well make up their minds first as last to work out their own salvation at the polls."[143]

Alma White founded the periodical *Woman's Chains* in 1924 as a forum for her feminist message. She outlined its purpose: *"Woman's Chains* is devoted to the interests of women's rights and is pleading that civilization will break all of her shackles and give to her her rightful place in the nation's religious, economic and industrial affairs, believing that numerous medieval laws and foolish customs hamper her."[144] Drawings by Pillar of Fire member Branford Clarke illustrated the periodical. Predominantly political in content, Clarke's sketches encouraged women to vote and run for office. Captions such as "Are you doing your duty as a voter?" and "Women use your vote" accompanied his illustrations.[145] Other drawings pictured specific inequalities and instances of discrimination that women experienced. Through his art work, Clarke also expressed the hope of a future day when equality would be realized.

Authors in *Woman's Chains* also encouraged women to vote. Kathleen White, Arthur's wife, appealed to women to use the ballot: "Many sacrifices have been made by women who suffered persecution even, because they espoused the cause of equal rights for women. Women today should cherish the privilege of the vote and use it in accordance with their best wisdom, and with those principles upon which our nation was founded."[146] Members of the National Woman's Party had experienced police brutality and imprisonment in their pursuit of suffrage. The least women could do now was to exercise the hard-won right to vote.

Pillar of Fire member Inez Garretson answered the charge that women would be neglecting other important duties when they voted, a concern that had been voiced years earlier by opponents of suffrage. Like the suffragists before her, Garretson contended that women would be able to handle voting along with their other responsibilities. She recommended that women take an interest in politics and elect the right people.[147] In order to remove any doubt about who the right people were, Pillar of Fire endorsed candidates. For instance, in the 1928 Republican primaries, it supported Mrs. Lillian Ford Feinckart for the U.S. Senate seat from New Jersey.[148]

Alma celebrated the victory of women's right to vote, but in her estimation voting represented minimal involvement in the affairs of government. Suffrage was not enough. She believed that "true democracy cannot be established upon the basis of inequality of the sexes. Those who govern must do so by the consent of those who are to be governed. Otherwise there can be no democracy. To exclude woman from taking any initiative or part in making the laws by which she is governed is tyranny."[149] She challenged the popular misconception that women and men had achieved equality by asking, "We hear much of woman's equality with man, but where are our women senators, where are our women judges, where are our women jurors?"[150]

Alma advocated women's participation at all levels of government. She believed that in court cases, a woman should face a jury of her peers. Pillar of Fire theologian L. S. Lawrence realized the experience would not always be pleasant for women but nonetheless maintained that they should serve as jurors. Appropriate involvement of women in government, though, involved more than jury duty. In an article entitled "What Can Women Do?," Pillar of Fire member Gertrude Wolfram answered the question asked in the title: "She can and should do anything and everything politically that men do."[151] An illustration in *Woman's Chains* depicted a woman scaling a mountain, overtaking several governmental occupations on her way to the White House at the top. With the assistance of women's votes, she conquered the following jobs as she traveled to the peak: school trustee, state legislator, mayor, U.S. Representative, U.S. Senator, governor, and Supreme Court justice.[152] Alma maintained that no position in government was outside women's reach. She anticipated a positive future in which every woman "will find her place, divinely appointed by her Creator, where she may cooperate with men in the administrations of human government."[153]

Besides preaching and writing articles in support of women's increased role in government, Alma authored at least one letter to a politician, Governor Sweet of Colorado, urging him to appoint a woman to fill a vacant U.S. Senate seat. She realized that the governor would probably disregard her letter, but she saw value in raising the issue of women's presence in the legislature.[154] This action illustrates Alma's commitment to the struggle for women's involvement in all areas of politics. Even though it was unlikely that her letter would make a difference in filling this particular vacancy, she was convinced that ultimately, with continued agitation, things would change.

Alma and the National Woman's Party constituted a vocal minority that contended for women's rights after 1920. Sharing Alma's conviction that women's equality was not realized with the passage of the suffrage amendment, the National Woman's Party turned its attention to a careful analysis of discriminatory laws. Women lawyers in its legal research department spent two years scouring law books, constitutions, and court decisions in every state, documenting the many laws that discriminated against women. Subsequent to its examination, the National Woman's Party decided the best means of abolishing these laws was to incorporate equality into the nation's law through adoption of the Equal Rights Amendment (ERA). It submitted the amendment to the judiciary committees of both houses of Congress in December 1923. The ERA stated simply that "men and women shall have equal rights throughout the United States and every place subject to its jurisdiction."[155] A member of the National Woman's Party stated the rationale for introducing and promoting this constitutional amendment:

> We are striving to remove every artificial handicap placed upon women by law and custom. . . . The amendment would at one stroke compel both federal and state governments to observe the principle of Equal Rights. It would override all existing legislation which denied women equal rights with men, and it would render invalid every future attempt to interfere with these rights.[156]

With one fell swoop, the passage of the Equal Rights Amendment would nullify all discriminatory laws.

Alma White endorsed the Equal Rights Amendment at its inception, expecting it to further advance equality between the sexes. The ultimate goal of Alma and the National Woman's Party was the realization of equality. The NWP believed passage of the Equal Rights Amendment would help them achieve their sole objective, which was "to remove all forms of the subjection of women."[157] In one article L. S. Lawrence asked, "Should We Have the ERA?" Reflecting Alma's perspective, his answer was unequivocal: "We trust the ERA will soon be an established fact, and that one-half of our population will come into possession of their rights."[158] Alma supported the ERA in order to achieve equality between the sexes as it was in the beginning when "God gave men and women copartnership and control of all that He had created."[159] Alma's promotion of the amendment, like her support of suffrage, rested on the belief that God favored women's equality. "Those who would discriminate between the sexes and rob women of their God-given rights are aliens to the cause," Alma contended, "and without knowledge of God's plan for the redemption of the world."[160]

The general historical consensus that the National Woman's Party stood alone when it introduced the Equal Rights Amendment is erroneous.[161] The Pillar of Fire deserves recognition as the only religious group to endorse the Equal Rights Amendment at its inception, yet no studies of the amendment acknowledge Alma's or her church's support. It is no coincidence that the first issue of *Woman's Chains* appeared in January 1924, less than one month after the amendment was submitted to Congress. Alma staunchly defended the necessity of the ERA. A Pillar of Fire member wrote the following report of a service at Zarephath in April 1924 during which Alma spoke on the amendment:

> The laws that discriminate against women were commented on by Bishop Alma White. Her statements were a great revelation to the listeners, and no doubt will be productive of much good in the reform movement that is on foot to remedy this monstrous evil. An Equal Rights bill is now before Congress and should have the support of every true American citizen.[162]

Alma made extensive use of information in National Woman's Party pamphlets and articles from its magazine *Equal Rights*. One department in *Woman's Chains*, "How the Laws of Various States Discriminate Against Women," highlighted a different state in each issue. Information came directly from National Woman's Party pamphlets, each of which summarized the results of legal research of the laws in one state. Alma also quoted from these pamphlets in her sermons. For example, at a service in Brooklyn, New York on December 26, 1923, she listed several laws discriminating against women in the state of New York. *Equal Rights* articles reprinted in *Woman's Chains* include "The Bogeyman Argument," reprinted in the July-August 1924 issue, and "The ERA," in the November-December 1924 issue.

Incomplete records make it impossible to verify Alma's membership in the National Woman's Party.[163] Whether or not she was a formal member, there is no doubt that she supported the National Woman's Party's agenda of promoting equality for women. An illustration in *Woman's Chains* pictured Uncle Sam opening the door to offer a member of the Woman's Party more offices in government.[164] *Woman's Chains* printed a press release, "What the National Woman's Party Has Done for Women in New Jersey 1925-1928," which summarized the passage of eight equal rights bills in New Jersey,[165] and kept its readership abreast of other National Woman's Party's achievements.

At least one National Woman's Party lecturer spoke at Zarephath.

Woman's Chains reported that Mary DuBrow's speech on the Equal Rights Amendment in 1924 was "very interesting and instructive." The news item also noted that "the chapel was well filled and the audience was appreciative."[166] Alma's followers shared her enthusiasm for the amendment.

Initially, no other women's organizations joined the National Woman's Party and Alma'a Pillar of Fire in support of the Equal Rights Amendment. Instead, many women's groups actively opposed the amendment even before it was officially introduced in Congress. As early as mid-1922, groups such as the Women's Trade Union League, the League of Women Voters, and the National Consumers' League went on record against the proposed amendment. The Women's Joint Congressional Committee, sponsored by twenty-one women's organizations at its peak, lobbied against the ERA.[167] Women in the New Deal network, for the most part, used their power and influence to thwart the amendment.[168]

Believing women needed special protection, social reformers of the 1920s and 1930s mobilized against the Equal Rights Amendment because it threatened to abolish protective labor legislation they had secured for women workers. Florence Kelley, a prominent reformer, contended: "Women cannot be made men by act of the legislature or by amendment to the Federal Constitution. The inherent differences are permanent. Women will always need many laws different from those needed by men."[169] Maintaining the opposite position, the National Woman's Party stressed the similarities between men and women and intended for the Equal Rights Amendment to protect all workers, not just women, from unhealthy work environments.[170] By aligning herself with the National Woman's Party, Alma placed herself in opposition to those who favored protective labor legislation for women.

Although the Equal Rights Amendment was initially unpopular not only with the majority of Americans but also with women's groups, support for the amendment slowly mounted. Gradually, other organizations admitted the actuality of women's inferior status under the law and ratified the ERA. Alma had recognized the wisdom of the National Woman's Party amendment from its inception.

Alma was a public feminist who based her demands for women's rights on the belief in women's inherent equality. If she had supported suffrage merely on the grounds of expediency, in order to implement a reform agenda, she would have shown no interest in the ERA. A shared commitment to female equality drew Alma and the National Woman's Party together. Realizing that men would not grant women equality merely for the asking, they advocated aggressive methods to accomplish their goal. Women must use the vote to contend for their rights and must play an increased role in government by filling all political offices. Undaunted by the opposition, Alma remained firmly convinced that women would achieve equality under the law only with passage of the Equal Rights Amendment.

CONTINUING MINISTRIES

{Alma White} lived to see her sect become a going concern and a factor in the life of several communities.
No one save a person of force, courage and determination could have accomplished that.

—*Obituary in Rocky Mountain News*

In her final years Alma continued her commitment to the ministries and political causes characteristic of her. She observed in 1932 that although women had voted for twelve years, their equality was far from a reality because laws discriminating against women still permeated state statute books.[171] Alma believed the fight for equality should continue until all such laws were overturned. Her daughter-in-law, Kathleen White, quoted information from NWP's *Equal Rights* in a 1944 article and concluded, "Again we declare that if women are now bearing equal responsibilities with men and are doing this wholeheartedly and willingly, it is time for them to be given equality with men before the law."[172]

Alma's sermon topics reflected her ongoing commitment to women's rights. Diary entries document that she preached on women's oppression, women's equality, discrimination between the sexes, women's place in the church, women's status in the Bible, discrimination, and the slavery of women. During February and March 1946 she spoke three times on the chains that enslave women. The last sermon she preached before her death included a plea for women's right to preach the gospel.[173] She firmly believed that ultimately women would secure their rights because "God is on the side of truth and justice" and justice demanded equality.[174]

Although Alma's interest in women's rights never subsided, her support of the Ku Klux Klan, which nevertheless extended beyond the Klan's rapid demise nationally in the mid-1920s, gradually diminished. In 1927, she or her members attended nineteen KKK meetings, and the following year they participated in eleven. The number of meetings averaged two a year in subsequent years, although Alma allowed the Klan in Denver to use her auditorium for their meetings. The periodical *Good Citizen,* which Alma had used to promote the Klan agenda, ceased publication in 1933.

In the same year, the Eighteenth Amendment, mandating prohibition of alcohol, was repealed, and Alma turned her energy to the temperance cause. She responded to this setback by inaugurating the magazine *Dry Legion* in 1934[175] Alma received national attention in 1939 and 1940 for two prohibition plays improvised by Pillar of Fire members from outlines she had written.[176] Pillar of Fire branches in Brooklyn, New York, and Boulder, Colorado sponsored "The Drunken Son's Revenge" and "Joe Sharpe, the Mission Drunk." About one thousand attended a performance in Denver on March 30, 1941. During this time, she distributed petitions in an attempt to get prohibition on the ballot.[177]

Alma's involvement in politics extended beyond support of prohibition and advocacy of the Equal Rights Amendment. In 1940, she attended the Republican National Convention and attempted to persuade the Colorado delegation to back Arthur Vandenburg. She also wrote letters to legislators, including the governor and congressmen from California, in an attempt to solicit their support in saving redwood trees. She often gave "election" speeches, advising her listeners regarding which candidates they should support. Alma generally voted a straight Republican ticket, and she lamented the Democratic victories at the state level in 1934 by writing that "Satan has the reins now."[178]

Alma dramatically extended her potential for evangelistic and political outreach when the Pillar of Fire received a license in 1927 from the Federal Radio Commission to operate a Denver AM station with call letters KPOF. Limited initially to 250 watts, KPOF's religious programming commenced March 9, 1928. Alma's son Ray described KPOF in a fund-raising letter: "It is not a commercial station; it sells no time; it broadcasts no jazz."[179] Contributions from listeners enabled the station to remain on the air.

Pillar of Fire purchased a second radio station (WAWZ), which began broadcasting from Zarephath in March 1931.[180] In 1941, the Pillar of Fire received permission to increase this station's power to five thousand watts, and the Denver station expanded to five thousand watts in 1945. Pillar of Fire claims to be the first church group to own and operate a network of affiliate religious radio stations. Alma took advantage of modern technology, revealing a wisdom and foresight absent among most of her contemporaries. Were Alma alive today, she probably would be a prominent television preacher with her own religious network.

A major milestone for the Pillar of Fire was the completion of Alma Temple in Denver. Alma purchased ten lots, less than one block from the state capitol, in 1923, and construction began the same year. Opened in 1926 with services conducted in the basement, construction ceased for several years due to the depression. The building's official dedication ceremony took place on October 31, 1937, when an audience of two thousand heard Denver mayor Benjamin Stapleton speak. Alma built the temple, a lava stone and light gray brick edifice, to serve as "a monument to the credit of our entire movement in the United States and across the seas."[181]

It is difficult to trace the development of Pillar of Fire branches other than Denver and Zarephath. One source indicated there were forty-nine branches in 1937, and another specified that there were sixty-one branches in 1946.[182] Arthur White wrote in 1948 that "some fifty branches of the society were organized."[183] A list itemized eighty-two properties, including churches, homes, and lots purchased between 1902 and Alma's death in 1946. One impressive transaction occurred in London in 1925 when Alma negotiated the purchase of an estate consisting of one hundred rooms. Many acquisitions resulted in the accumulation of land adjacent to the Denver and Zarephath properties. The combined purchase price for these transactions was $620,314.34.[184]

The value of the properties was often much more than the purchase price. For instance, Alma purchased a house in St. Louis for $5,500 and sold it three years later for $36,000—then applied the profit toward the purchase of the temple site in Denver. Besides the difficulty in assessing the fluctuation in the number of branches, it is hard to ascertain when various Pillar of Fire schools operated. It is known that seven schools opened in Colorado during the 1930s and eighteen were established throughout the United States during the 1940s.[185] Comprehensive membership statistics during Alma's lifetime have been unavailable. *The Yearbook of American Churches* listed fifty-one hundred members in 1948.[186]

Alma maintained close supervision over her branches and membership. Intimately involved in the most mundane decisions relating to the Pillar of Fire, she never functioned as a mere figurehead. Determining staff placements was a primary concern, but Alma also furnished the branch homes, in some cases down to the curtains and dishes. She also supervised house cleaning, plumbing work, and tearing up carpeting during her visits. She even advised pruners at Zarephath which branches they should trim. She bargained for cars that she then assigned to the various branches (the Pillar of Fire owned nineteen cars in 1929). She rejoiced in receiving reduced prices, whether for automobiles or other necessary items.

Alma devoted a significant amount of time to answering her mail, dictating replies to various members who served as her secretaries. Although not providing a tally of her correspondence, she did indicate that on one day in 1931 she received nearly one hundred letters. Just two months prior to her death, she spoke of the need to answer her many letters.

Alma commuted frequently between Zarephath and Denver. In 1931, she made eight round trips between the two branches, visiting Cincinnati three times en route. She also took a personal interest in her other branches around the country, traveling to Brooklyn, Washington, D.C., Greeley, St. Louis, Salt Lake City, and Trenton during the same year. In 1945, she made six trips from Zarephath to Denver. In spite of illness during two months of 1945, she also visited branches in Salt Lake City, Los Angeles, San Francisco, Jacksonville, Colorado Springs, and Boulder.

Whenever problems emerged, whether on an individual level or involving all the members of a local branch, Alma would call a "prayer siege." She expected the party or parties involved to pray until they recognized and admitted their shortcomings. Alma attributed any difficulties she encountered, be they physical ailments or the inability to preach, to a lack of prayer on the part of her followers.

People who disagreed with Alma were "blocking the wheels." She believed that members who refused to follow her orders or who ultimately left the group were not genuine Christians. Alma told one disaffected member that there were "no walls or bars" compelling him to stay and offered to pay his travel expenses to any city in the country.[187] She did not want members who challenged her leadership or who were disrespectful.

Alma boycotted services as a rebuke to her people when they failed to measure up to her expectations. Members' absences from prayer meetings or failure to follow her instructions were shortcomings that could result in a boycott. Once she refused to speak when the personnel who were to sit on the platform at the Bound Brook church arrived late.[188]

For the most part, Alma worked amicably with her sons as they began to assume some of the responsibilities related to overseeing the Pillar of Fire. Alma believed that Arthur and Ray were good preachers, and she was proud of them. During the 1920s, they assumed the titles of first and second assistant superintendents, respectively. Alma and her sons did not always agree on every issue, though, and she documented several conflicts in her diary. For instance, she challenged Arthur's desire that Pillar of Fire members be allowed to wear wrist watches before finally acquiescing.[189] In matters of dress, Ray objected to the requirement that women wear high shoes. When Ray protested against the shoes, with his wife in mind, Alma "blew up" and "gave him such a lecturing as he has never had." The lecture did not prevent Ray from criticizing his mother later in 1937 when he advised her to tone down her preaching on Hitler.[190]

A major quarrel between Alma and Ray occurred in 1933. On December 19, Ray met with her because he had "something he had to get off his mind." Alma never revealed the issue that precipitated the controversy, but Ray's "outburst" resulted in "a day of Crucifixion" for Alma, after which she decided to resign as active head of the Pillar of Fire.[191] She sent copies of her resignation to Zarephath and Denver. Members at both locations refused to accept her resignation. Leaders in Denver urged her to reconsider, and ninety-four members in Zarephath voted unanimously to retain her as head of the church. In light of the positive affirmation, Alma withdrew her resignation. Apparently, she and Ray were able to settle their differences and continue working together.

In 1940, Arthur invited his father to come stay with him in Denver. Kent, who had moved to Toronto from England in 1939 to pastor an Apostolic Faith church, had a severe throat ailment in which a sac had formed on his esophagus. There is no indication that Arthur consulted with Alma before communicating with his father, and her views on Arthur's invitation are unknown. Alma, who was in Denver when Kent arrived, had not seen him since a brief visit in Brooklyn in 1922. They had rarely communicated since then, and she apparently had accepted

Kent's assessment of their relationship: "Why hitch up two horses again that are contrary and will not pull together? Better they work single and far apart."[192] After the 1922 meeting, Kent had determined there was no chance of reconciliation.[193] Upon his arrival in Denver on July 4, 1940, Kent visited Alma and put his arms around her. After the many years of contention, they still cared for each other. When Alma decided to travel to Zarephath, Kent begged Ray to use his influence to convince her to stay. Alma left after recording in her diary, "It is too late after his 25 years of separation to tell me what to do."[194] Alma was gone from July 18 until July 26, the day Kent was scheduled for an operation. In spite of the operation, Kent died on July 30, 1940, at age seventy-nine. In his funeral sermon, Ray shared that his father had come to Denver to be reconciled with his family whether or not they embraced the doctrine of glossolalia.[195]

As she grew older, Alma maintained her close control and supervision over the Pillar of Fire. An article documented her busy schedule at age seventy-five:

> Bishop White, who is past her three score and ten but is still blest with the dynamic energy of a dozen that astonishes the world. With a preaching itinerancy that would push the Apostle Paul's straight off the New Testament map, she traveled some 45,000 miles last year, buying property, raising money, and urging people to conform to the ways of the Lord. She sometimes preaches twenty-one sermons a week, five on Sunday. She also edits six Pillar of Fire journals.[196]

Alma's writing responsibilities included revising earlier books, compiling her autobiographies, and completing the fifth volume of *The Story of My Life and the Pillar of Fire* in 1943.

Her creative impulses were not limited to the pen. Alma had begun oil painting after age seventy and painted more than three hundred pictures by 1940. Morton Gallery in New York sponsored three exhibits of her work.[197] Admitting that it was a relaxing pastime, she also worked with a pragmatic agenda in mind. She decorated the walls of Pillar of Fire homes with her paintings, which were primarily nature scenes, and believed they were a future investment in that the Pillar of Fire could sell them after her death.

On February 1, 1940, Alma, now seventy-seven, wrote in her diary that she could not "go all day as I have in the past." Three weeks later, however, she reported that she had preached four times in the same day. Popular sermon topics included temperance, women's issues, national and international affairs, and tirades against Catholicism and pentecostalism. She frequently described her sermons as being "hot" or "on fire." Referring to a sermon she preached on December 30, 1945, Alma observed, "I had the holy fire on me until I was aflame." Although she inevitably was slowing down due to age, Alma possessed enough energy to broadcast a sermon lasting one hour and fifteen minutes over the Zarephath radio station March 2, 1946.

Alma White presided over the Pillar of Fire church until her death on June 26, 1946, at age eighty-four of arteriosclerotic heart disease. Her remains were flown from Zarephath to Denver because Arthur could not bear the thought of accompanying his mother's remains on the train, a trip they had so often made together. She was buried, according to her instructions, between plots reserved for her two sons rather than next to Kent, who was also interred at Fairmount Cemetery.

Epilog

Following Alma's death, Arthur, who had been consecrated bishop in 1932, became the second president and general superintendent of Pillar of Fire. Arthur had controlled the church alone since Ray's death in 1946, the same year as his mother's. In 1978, Arthur's daughter, Arlene White Lawrence, assumed the leadership position. Donald Wolfram has been president since 1984.

Commitment to feminism in the Pillar of Fire outlived Alma. Arthur praised the National Woman's Party positively as late as 1963: "There is still a great organization contending equal constitutional and state rights for women."[1] In interviews, Pillar of Fire members consistently emphasize that their church has ordained women since its inception and recommend Lee Anna Starr's *The Bible Status of Woman* (which they reprinted in 1955) to indicate their ongoing commitment to women clergy.

Alma's publications, like Starr's, provide a biblical hermeneutic that support women's autonomy. Although most people limited its application to the church, Alma extended it to the state, devoting her ministry to the fight for women's autonomy in both areas. Alma's life can best be understood as a quest to achieve autonomy and to maintain it in the face of serious threats from those who sought to place her or her church under their control.

Alma's social analysis of the patriarchal power structure parallels current feminist theory. She understood that women face a formidable male power structure as they seek equal rights:

> But man, for the most part, has unchained his bulldogs and placed them to guard the gates where perchance women might find an entrance to the pulpits or to the halls of legislation. Men have charge of the gates, own the bulldogs, and their keepers, too, and any woman who tries to catch them off their guard, rise above her present status and press her way in, will have a difficult task.[2]

Rather than overwhelming the bulldogs and crashing through the gates, Alma established the Pillar of Fire, creating an autonomous space in which she fought to dismantle all barriers preventing women from achieving equality. This was her task. And her legacy continues today.

Notes

ACKNOWLEDGMENTS

1. Donald W. Dayton and Lucille Sider Dayton, "Recovering a Heritage: Part II—Evangelical Feminism," *Post-American,* August–September 1974, 9.

2. Carolyn G. Heilbrun, *Writing a Woman's Life* (New York: Ballantine Books, 1988), 46.

INTRODUCTION

1. William L. O'Neill, *Everyone Was Brave: A History of Feminism in America* (New York: Quadrangle/New York Times Book Co., 1969), vii.

2. "A Woman Bishop," *Woman's Outlook,* January 1922, in *Alma White's Evangelism: Press Reports,* 2 vols., ed. C. R. Paige and C. K. Ingler (Zarephath, N.J.: Pillar of Fire, 1939–40), 1:222.

3. Lee Casey, "Bishop White of Denver—A Cromwell in Skirts," *Denver Rocky Mountain News,* 28 June 1946, 14.

4. Alma White, *The Story of My Life and the Pillar of Fire,* 5 vols. (Zarephath, N.J.: Pillar of Fire, 1935–43), 5:132.

5. Nancy F. Cott, *The Bonds of Womanhood: "Women's Sphere" in New England, 1780–1835* (New Haven: Yale University Press, 1977), 140. Cott documented Christianity's role during the late eighteenth and early nineteenth centuries in enabling women to challenge society's limitations on their gender. Alma White stands in the tradition of women such as Ann Hutchinson and Sarah Grimké, whom Cott credits with displaying "the subversive potential of religious belief."

6. Alma White, "Woman's Place," in *Radio Sermons and Lectures* (Denver: Pillar of Fire, 1936), 208.

7. Donald W. Dayton, "Prophesying Daughters: The Ministry of Women in the Holiness Movement" (Paper presented at the United Methodist Church Conference "Women in New Worlds," Cincinnati, 1980).

8. Nancy Hardesty, Lucille Sider Dayton, and Donald W. Dayton, "Women in the Holiness Movement: Feminism in the Evangelical Tradition," in *Women of Spirit: Female Leadership in the Jewish and Christian Traditions,* ed. Rosemary Ruether and Eleanor McLaughlin (New York: Simon and Schuster, 1979), 244.

9. The Methodist Episcopal church (now the United Methodist church) as well as the Protestant Episcopal church, the Presbyterian church, and the various Lutheran churches were among the groups that refused to ordain women

at the turn of the century.

10. Robert Stanley Ingersol, "Burden of Dissent: Mary Lee Cagle and the Southern Holiness Movement" (Ph.D. diss., Duke University, 1989), 284, 298.

11. "Record of the Woman's Ministerial Conference," 84, quoted in Cynthia Grant Tucker, *Prophetic Sisterhood: Liberal Women Ministers of the Frontier, 1880–1930* (Boston: Beacon Press, 1990), 58. This figure does not include the Society of Friends (Quakers), who record their clergy rather than ordain them. In 1889 there were approximately 350 women recorded by the Friends. Ada C. Bowles, "Woman in the Ministry," in *Woman's Work in America,* ed. Annie Nathan Miller (New York: Henry Holt and Co., 1891; reprint, New York: Arno Press, 1972), 207.

12. "Women Preachers," *Woman Citizen,* December 1920, 796, 802.

13. The percentages are derived from 1986 statistics compiled by Constant H. Jacquet, Jr., *Women Ministers in 1986 and 1977: A Ten Year View* (New York: Office of Research and Evaluation, National Council of Churches, 1988), 5–6. The five Wesleyan/Holiness groups are Church of God (Anderson, Indiana), Church of the Nazarene, Free Methodist church, Salvation Army, and Wesleyan church.

14. Alma White, *The New Testament Church* (Denver: Pillar of Fire, 1907; rev., Zarephath. N.J.: Pillar of Fire, 1929), 277.

15. "Girl Rises from Kentucky Farm to Bishop," in Paige and Ingler, *Alma White's Evangelism,* 1:39.

16. Alma White, "Commencement at Zarephath," *Woman's Chains,* July–August 1927, 2.

17. Esther Coster, "Only Woman Bishop Founded Pillar of Fire Church," *Brooklyn Daily Eagle,* 30 December 1939, in Paige and Ingler, *Alma White's Evangelism,* 2:269.

18. George Marsden, *Fundamentalism and American Culture: The Shaping of Twentieth-Century Evangelicalism 1870–1925* (Oxford: Oxford University Press, 1980), 4. For an examination of the fundamentalist/modernist debate, consult this book and William R. Hutchinson, *The Modernist Impulse in American Protantism* (Oxford: Oxford University Press, 1976).

19. Jean Miller Schmidt applied this phrase to groups that did not enter into the fundamentalist/modernist debate. Jean Miller Schmidt, *Souls or the Social Order: The Two-Party System in American Protestantism* (Brooklyn: Carlson Publishing, 1991), 173–96.

20. For more information on this transition within the Wesleyan/Holiness movement, consult Kenneth O. Brown, "Leadership in the National Holiness Association with Special Reference to Eschatology, 1867–1919" (Ph.D. diss., Drew University, 1988).

21. Esther Coster, "Only Woman Bishop," in Paige and Ingler, *Alma White's Evangelism,* 2:269–70.

22. Martin E. Marty, *Modern American Religion,* vol. 1 of *The Irony of It All 1893–1919* (Chicago: University of Chicago Press, 1986), 237.

23. Alma White, *The New Testament Church,* 39.

24. Ibid., 22.

25. Margaret Lamberts Bendroth, "Fundamentalism and Femininity: Points of Encounter Between Religious Conservatives and Women, 1919–1935," *Church History* 61 (June 1992): 222. Neither Bendroth nor Betty A. DeBerg (*Ungodly Women: Gender and the First Wave of American Fundamentalism* [Philadelphia: Augsburg/Fortress, 1990]) discuss Alma White in their analyses of fundamentalism and gender.

26. Carolyn G. Heilbrun, *Writing a Woman's Life*, 118.

27. Notable examples are Susan D. Becker, *The Origins of the Equal Rights Amendment: American Feminism Between the Wars* (Westport, Conn.: Greenwood Press, 1981) and Nancy F. Cott, *The Grounding of Modern Feminism* (New Haven: Yale University Press, 1987). Cott's book is a history of the National Woman's Party and feminism between 1910 and 1930. Neither author mentions Alma.

CHAPTER I

1. Alma's siblings and their dates of birth are as follows: Martha Gertrude, March 18, 1852; James Robert, December 16, 1853; Emery Bascom, February 14, 1856; Amanda Frances, May 31, 1857; Ann Eliza [Lida], December 16, 1858; Venora Ella [Nora], January 18, 1861; Theresa West, August 16, 1864; Laura Kate, February 22, 1866; Rollie Taylor, September 3, 1868; and Charles William, July 25, 1872. Alma White, *Story* (1935–43), 1:9.

2. Ibid., 1:11, 44.

3. Ibid., 1:13.

4. Ibid., 1:11, 115.

5. Ibid., 1:69–70.

6. Merton Coulter, *The Civil War and Readjustment in Kentucky* (Gloucester, Mass.: Peter Smith, 1966), 400. The geographical schism ended with the reunion of the two groups in 1939.

7. Alma White, *The Story of My Life and the Pillar of Fire*, 6 vols. (Zarephath, N.J.: Pillar of Fire, 1919–34), 1:140.

8. White, *Story* (1935–43), 1:117.

9. Virginia Lieson Brereton, *From Sin to Salvation: Stories of Women's Conversions, 1800 to the Present* (Bloomington: Indiana University Press, 1991), 5–6.

10. Alma's recollection of pastoral changes in Vanceburg was inconsistent and faulty. In one book, she lists J. S. Sims, J. M. Carter, and W. B. Godbey, in that order, as pastors. Alma White, *Looking Back from Beulah* (Denver: Pentecostal Union, 1902; reprint, Zarephath, N.J.: Pillar of Fire, 1951), 20–22. In another source, she lists J. M. Carter, then J. S. Sims, followed by W. B. Godbey. White, *Story* (1935–43), 1:139, 140, 153. An examination of Methodist Episcopal conference records reveals that J. S. Sims served the Vanceburg church in 1876 and 1877. W. B. Godbey pastored the Vanceburg church in 1878, followed by J. M. Carter in 1879. *Minutes of the Fifty-Sixth Session of the Kentucky Annual Conference of the Methodist Episcopal Church, South Held in Nicholasville, Ky., September 13–19, 1876* (Louisville: John P. Morton and Company, 1876), 15; *Minutes of the Fifty-Seventh Session of the Kentucky Annual Conference of the Methodist Episcopal Church, South Held in Winchester,*

Ky., September 5–12, 1877 (Louisville: John P. Morton and Company, 1877), 16; Minutes of the Fifty-Eighth Session of the Kentucky Annual Conference of the Methodist Episcopal Church, South Held in Shelbyville, Ky., September 18–25, 1878 (Louisville: John P. Morton and Company, 1878), 11; and Minutes of the Fifty-Ninth Session of the Kentucky Annual Conference of the Methodist Episcopal Church, South Held in Richmond, Ky., September 17–23, 1879 (Louisville: John P. Morton and Company, 1879), 12.

11. White, Story (1935–43), 1:145, 144.

12. "Memoirs: Rev. W. B. Godbey, D.D." Journal Kentucky Conference: Methodist Episcopal Church, South 1921, 70, 69, 72.

13. Ibid., 73.

14. White, Story (1919–34), 1:223–24.

15. White, Story (1935–43), 1:161.

16. "May Women Preach?" Quarterly Review of the Methodist Episcopal Church, South, n.s. 3 (July 1881): 479.

17. White, Story (1935–43), 1:161.

18. Barbara Welter, "She Hath Done What She Could: Protestant Women's Missionary Careers in Nineteenth-Century America," in Women in American Religion, ed. Janet Wilson James (Philadelphia: University of Pennsylvania Press, 1980), 119.

19. For documentation of the activities of the Woman's Missionary Society in China between 1880 and 1900, see Adrian A. Bennett, "Doing More Than They Intended," in Women in New Worlds, ed. Rosemary Skinner Keller, Louise L. Queen, and Hilah F. Thomas (Nashville: Abingdon Press, 1982), 2:249–67.

20. White, Story (1935–43), 1:182. Godbey authored a defense of women preachers in 1891. William Godbey, Woman Preacher (Atlanta: Office of the Way of Life, 1891). If he supported women clergy at the time he advised Alma, perhaps he discouraged her aspirations in an attempt to protect her from the virulent opposition she would surely face as a woman preacher.

21. Leonard I. Sweet, The Minister's Wife: Her Role in Nineteenth Century American Evangelicalism (Philadelphia: Temple University Press, 1983), 3.

22. White, Story (1935–43), 1:196–97.

23. White, Musings of the Past (Zarephath, N.J.: Pillar of Fire, 1927), 95–96.

24. White, Story (1935–43), 1:250.

25. White, Story (1919–34), 1:287.

26. White, Story (1935–43), 1:235.

27. Ibid., 1:269–70.

28. Ibid., 1:279.

29. Alma refers to this town as Luna in Looking Back from Beulah, 102. This is obviously a typographical error.

30. Accounts in both editions of Story reported that their initial meeting occurred on March 31, 1883. White, Story (1919–34), 2:53. In Looking Back from Beulah (p. 61), Alma stated that the first meeting occurred on March 3, 1883. Kent White's diary and Kent White, "Early Important Dates in My Life" (N.p., n.d.) confirm the March 3 date.

31. White, "Early Important Dates in My Life."

32. White, *Story* (1935–43), 1:236.

33. In 1892, the Iliff School of Theology became a separate entity from the University of Denver, which today continues as a liberal arts school.

34. White, *Story* (1935–43), 1:236.

35. Kent White to Mollie Bridwell, 20 November 1886.

36. Mollie Bridwell to Kent White, 28 November 1886.

37. Kent White's journal, quoted in White, *Story* (1935–43), 1:285. In the early 1900s, she dropped "Mollie" and referred to herself thenceforth as "Alma."

38. Kent White to Mollie Bridwell, 8 April 1887.

39. White, *Story* (1919–34), 2:170.

40. Ibid., 2:171.

41. White, *Story* (1935–43), 1:308.

42. Ibid., 2:313, 1:319.

43. Ibid., 1:345, 346.

44. White, *Story* (1919–34), 2:235; White, *Story* (1935–43), 1:350, 345.

45. Isaac Haight Beardsley, *Echoes from Peak and Plain; or, Tales of Life, War, Travel, and Colorado Methodism* (Cincinnati: Curts & Jennings, 1898), 515.

46. Alma rarely spoke of her children in her autobiographies other than to mention their illnesses as babies.

CHAPTER 2

1. White, *Story* (1935–43), 1:354.

2. Lillian Pool, "Experience and Call to the Ministry," in *Women Preachers,* ed. Fanny McDowell Hunter (Dallas: Berachah Printing, 1905), 67; Sarah Smith, *Life Sketches of Mother Sarah Smith* (Anderson, Ind.: Gospel Trumpet Company, [1902]; reprint, Guthrie, Okla.: Faith Publishing House, n.d.), 9.

3. John Wesley, *A Plain Account of Christian Perfection* (London, 1872; reprint, Kansas City, Mo.: Beacon Hill Press of Kansas City, 1966), 61.

4. Ibid.

5. Terry D. Bilhartz, comp. and ed., *Francis Asbury's America: An Album of Early American Methodism* (Grand Rapids, Mich.: Francis Asbury Press of Zondervan Publishing House, 1984), 82.

6. The following biographies detail Palmer's life. Charles Edward White, *Beauty of Holiness* (Grand Rapids, Mich.: Francis Asbury Press of Zondervan, 1986) and Harold E. Raser, *Phoebe Palmer: Her Life and Thought* (Lewiston, N.Y.: Edwin Mellon Press, 1987).

7. Nancy A. Hardesty, "'Your Daughters Shall Prophesy:' Revivalism and Feminism in the Age of Finney" (Ph.D. diss., University of Chicago, 1976), 45, 48–49.

8. Phoebe Palmer, *The Way of Holiness with Notes by the Way; Being a Narrative of Religious Experience Resulting from a Determination to be a Bible Christian* (New York: Piercy and Reed, 1843; reprint, Salem, Ohio: Schmul Publishing, 1988), 46.

9. Ibid., 15.

10. For a discussion of this difference between Wesley's and Palmer's understanding of holiness, see Ivan Howard, "Wesley vs. Phoebe Palmer: An Extended Controversy," *Wesleyan Theological Journal* 11 (Spring 1971): 31–40.

11. Palmer, *Way of Holiness,* 87.

12. Timothy L. Smith, *Revivalism and Social Reform in Mid-Nineteenth Century America* (New York: Abingdon Press, 1957; reprint, with new title *Revivalism and Social Reform: American Protestantism on the Eve of the Civil War,* Baltimore: Johns Hopkins University Press, 1980), 114–34. For a discussion of holiness in the United States between 1766 and 1866, see chapter 1 of Vinson Synan, *The Holiness-Pentecostal Movement in the United States* (Grand Rapids, Mich.: William B. Eerdmans Publishing, 1971).

13. Beardsley, *Echoes from Peak and Plain,* 515.

14. White, *Story* (1935–43), 1:230

15. Ibid., 1:239.

16. Mollie Bridwell to Kent White, 10 November 1883.

17. William B. Godbey, *Victory* (Cincinnati: M. W. Knapp, 1888).

18. White, *Story* (1935–43), 1:397.

19. Ibid., 1:410, 2:206.

20. Phoebe Palmer, *The Promise of the Father; or, A Neglected Specialty of the Last Days* (Boston: Henry V. Degen, 1859; reprint, Salem, Ohio: Schmul Publishers, n.d.), 245.

21. Phoebe Palmer, *Entire Devotion to God* (n.p., n.d.; reprint, Salem, Ohio: Schmul Publishers, n.d.), 21.

22. White, *Looking Back from Beulah,* 172.

23. White, *Story* (1935–43), 1:412.

24. White, *Looking Back from Beulah,* 219.

25. Alma White, *Modern Miracles and Answers to Prayer* (Zarephath, N.J.: Pillar of Fire, 1939), 62.

26. Caroline Staats, interview with author, Denver, Colorado, 14 December 1981. See also Alma White, *Gems of Life: Short Selections for Children* (Bound Brook, N.J.: Pillar of Fire, 1907), 79.

27. White, *Looking Back from Beulah,* 182. See also 198.

28. White, *Modern Miracles,* 63.

29. White, *Story* (1935–43), 1:418.

30. Anne C. Loveland, "Domesticity and Religion in the Antebellum Period: The Career of Phoebe Palmer," *Historian,* May 1977:458–60, 465.

31. White, *Modern Miracles,* 68.

32. White, *Story* (1935–43), 2:12. Other officers were A. C. Peck, supervisor of the Haymarket Mission in Denver, and F. E. Yoakum, who served as president and vice president.

33. For a brief history of the National Camp-Meeting Association for the Promotion of Holiness, which emerged from this meeting, see chapter 3 of Charles E. Jones, *Perfectionist Persuasion: The Holiness Movement and American Methodism, 1867–1936,* ATLA Monograph Series, no. 5 (Metuchen, N.J.: Scarecrow Press, 1974) and also chapter 1 of Brown, "Leadership in the National Holiness Association."

34. Melvin Easterday Dieter, *The Holiness Revival of the Nineteenth Century,*

Studies in Evangelism, no. 1 (Metuchen, N.J.: Scarecrow Press, 1980), 117.

35. William B. Godbey, *Autobiography of Rev. W. B. Godbey, A.m.* (Cincinnati: God's Revivalist Office, 1909), 96. Godbey described his sanctification in "Experience of Dr. W. B. Godbey, Evangelist of Kentucky," *Guide to Holiness,* December 1896, 222–23.

36. "Memoirs: Rev. W. B. Godbey, D.D.," *Journal Kentucky Conference Methodist Episcopal Church, South 1921,* 70–71.

37. White, *Story* (1919–34), 3:76. She mentioned Arthur's presence in this source and in *Story* (1935–43), 2:55. In other accounts, Alma said they left in July (White, *Looking Back from Beulah,* 241) and both Ray and Arthur remained at home (Alma White, *Truth Stranger than Fiction* [Zarephath, N.J.: The Pentecostal Union (Pillar of Fire), 1913], 48).

38. White, *Truth Stranger than Fiction,* 51, 48.

39. White, *Story* (1935–43), 2:99.

40. *Journal of the Thirty-third Session of the Colorado Annual Conference of the Methodist Episcopal Church Held at Denver, Colorado June 6 to 11, 1895* (Denver: Dove Printer, 1895), 277.

41. "Monthly Review: The Home Field," *Guide to Holiness,* November 1895, 158. Founded in 1839, Phoebe Palmer owned and edited this magazine from 1858 until her death in 1874.

42. White, *Story* (1935–43), 2:74.

43. Ibid., 2:75.

44. Ibid., 2:73.

45. White, *Looking Back from Beulah,* 275.

46. White, *Story* (1935–43), 2:94. Alma consistently misspelled her name as "Vorn Holtz."

47. Gertrude Metlen Wolfram, *The Widow of Zarephath: A Church in the Making* (Zarephath, N.J.: Pillar of Fire, 1954), 8–9.

48. White, *Story* (1935–43), 2:70.

49. Ibid., 2:40.

50. Not all pastors anathematized Alma. Isaac Beardsley, a Methodist pastor and historian of early Methodism in Colorado, was sympathetic to both the holiness movement and the Whites's ministry. He commented positively on the Pleasant View camp meeting of 1894 and later camp meetings in Fort Collins. He also noted other Methodist clergy who preached holiness. Beardsley, *Echoes of Peak and Plain,* 516, 451, 508, 522, 526, 529, 541–42.

51. White, *Story* (1935–43), 2:30.

52. Ibid., 2:79.

53. Ibid., 2:80.

54. Ibid., 2:133–34.

55. Alma White, *Woman's Ministry* (London: Pillar of Fire, [1921]), 11, 15–16. See also Catherine Booth, *Female Ministry: Woman's Right to Preach the Gospel* (N.p., 1859; reprint, New York: Salvation Army Supplies Printing and Publishing Department, 1975), 12–13 and Godbey, *Woman Preacher,* 11.

56. White, *Story* (1935–43), 3:237.

57. Catherine Booth, Phoebe Palmer, and B. T. Roberts are among other holiness believers who agreed with this interpretation. Booth, *Female Minis-*

try, 8, 11; Palmer, *Promise of the Father,* 47, 6; and Benjamin Titus Roberts, *Ordaining Women* (Rochester, N.Y.: Earnest Christian Publishing House, 1891), 66–67.

58. Alma's argument was based on the definition of prophesying in 1 Corinthians 14:3: "He who prophesies speaks to men for their upbuilding and encouragement and consolation." White, *Story* (1935–43), 5:284.

59. A sampling of those who shared this view includes Palmer, *Promise of the Father,* 34, 43–44; Godbey, *Woman Preacher,* 8; Booth, *Female Ministry,* 7; and Roberts, *Ordaining Women,* 63.

60. White, *Story* (1935–43), 2:237.

61. Alma White, "Women in the New Testament," *Woman's Chains,* March–April 1941, 4.

62. White, *Woman's Ministry,* 7.

63. Roberts, *Ordaining Women,* 55.

64. White, *Woman's Ministry,* 8, 12–14.

65. Ibid., 12.

66. For example, see "'First Woman Preacher' Is Subject of Lecture," *Cincinnati Commercial Tribune,* 2 July 1921, Paige and Ingler, *Alma White's Evangelism,* 1:193; and White, *Story* (1935–43), 3:360.

67. White, *Woman's Ministry,* 4.

68. White, "Women in the New Testament," 5.

69. Booth, *Female Ministry,* 16; and Palmer, *Promise of the Father,* 14.

70. White, *Woman's Ministry,* 2.

71. Holiness exegetes pointed out the mistranslations of Romans 16 that had diminished the status of women. In some versions of the Bible, Phoebe is described as a servant, which is a mistranslation of *diakonos.* Roberts, *Ordaining Women,* 96. Junia is sometimes rendered incorrectly as "Junias." Palmer, *Promise of the Father,* 26.

72. "St. Paul's Attitude Toward Women," *Jacksonville Times-Union,* 21 May 1922, in Paige and Ingler, *Alma White's Evangelism,* 1:230.

73. John Leland Peters, *Christian Perfection and American Methodism* (New York: Abingdon Press, 1956), 138.

74. White, *Truth Stranger than Fiction,* 128.

75. Miranda L. Vorn Holz, *The Old Paths* (Cincinnati: M. W. Knapp, [1898]), chaps. 15 and 17.

76. Ibid., 361.

77. The People's Tabernacle was under the auspices of the Congregational church. Its holiness orientation stemmed from the fact that Rev. Uzzell's background was Methodist. Holiness doctrine permeated many denominations.

78. White, *Story* (1935–43), 2:95.

79. Ibid., 2:107.

80. Ibid., 2:99.

81. Ibid., 2:178.

82. Alma's use of typologies was popular in the Wesleyan/Holiness movement. For a recent example, see John F. Hay, "The Book of Jonah Preaches Holiness," *God's Revivalist and Bible Advocate,* January 1991, 14–15. The

author concludes his article: "The book of Jonah, like the text of all of the Bible, teaches holiness of heart and life" (15).

83. White, *Story* (1935–43), 2:35.
84. Ibid., 2:64.
85. Ibid., 2:65.
86. Ibid., 2:87.
87. Ibid., 2:122.
88. Ibid., 2:123.
89. White, *Story* (1919–34), 3:186–87.
90. White, *Story* (1935–43), 2:125.
91. White, *Truth Stranger than Fiction*, 125.
92. White, *Story* (1935–43), 2:153.
93. Ibid., 2:103.
94. White, *Modern Miracles*, 73–74.
95. White, *Story* (1935–43), 2:12.
96. Ibid., 2:177
97. Ibid., 2:180–81.
98. Ibid., 2:185.
99. Jernigan returned home and founded the Independent Holiness churches, which through a series of mergers with other groups eventuated in the Pentecostal Church of the Nazarene, now known as the Church of the Nazarene.
100. Knapp was a principal founder of the International Apostolic Holiness Union and Prayer League in 1897. The group eventually evolved into the Pilgrim Holiness church, which merged with the Wesleyan Methodist church in 1968 to become the Wesleyan church.
101. Merrill Elmer Gaddis, "Christian Perfectionism in America" (Ph.D. diss., University of Chicago, 1929), 458.
102. "Woman Bishop to Conduct Services in Manitou Now," *Colorado Springs Gazette*, July 1922.
103. White, *Story* (1935–43), 2:364.
104. Ibid., 2:228.
105. Ibid., 2:208.
106. White, *Modern Miracles*, 232.

CHAPTER 3

1. White, *Truth Stranger than Fiction*, 237.
2. Amanda Porterfield, *Feminine Spirituality in America: From Sarah Edwards to Martha Graham* (Philadelphia: Temple University Press, 1980), 21.
3. Charles A. Johnson, *The Frontier Camp Meeting: Religion's Harvest Time* (Dallas: Southern Methodist University Press, 1955), 59.
4. White, *The New Testament Church*, 339.
5. "Jump for Another Month," *Denver Times*, 5 August 1902, 3.
6. White, *Story* (1935–43), 2:240–41.
7. Ibid., 2:302, 296.

8. "Jumpers Jailed for Street Disturbance," *Denver Republic,* 9 February 1903, 10.

9. "'Jumpers' Jumped and Judge Thomas Lectured," *Denver Post,* 9 February 1903, 2.

10. White, *Story* (1919–34), 4:155.

11. Information on the building, officially called the Pentecostal Union Bible School and Missionary Training Home, came from an advertisement for the later sale of the property.

12. White, *Story* (1935–43), 2:309.

13. "Riot in Church Leads to Arrest of 4 Persons," *Salt Lake Telegraph,* 11 April 1904.

14. White, *Story* (1935–43), 2:343.

15. "'Jumpers' Queer Rites," *Denver Times,* 27 July 1902.

16. Ibid.

17. "Prayer and Faith Alleged to Have Restored a Woman's Sight—Hundreds Give up their All under Spur of Religious Fervor," *Denver Post,* 5 August 1902, 1.

18. "Exciting Revival," *Attleboro Sun* (Massachusetts), 27 December 1902; "Hell and Damnation," *Attleboro Sun* (Massachusetts), 24 December 1902.

19. "Denver Woman Who Is Creating Sensation in East," *Denver Times,* 29 December 1902, 5.

20. "Pentecostal Dancers," *Daily Mail* (London), 2 December 1904; *Daily Mail* (London), n.d.

21. "The Light Fantastic," *News of the World* (London), 4 December 1904.

22. "Cake Walk Chaos," *Daily Express* (London), 8 December 1904.

23. "The Holy Jumpers—Another New Religion," photocopy without name of newspaper, n.d.

24. "Holy Jiggery," *Star* (London), 6 December 1904; *Merthyr Express* (London), 25 March 1905.

25. "'Red Hot' Revival Services," *South London Observer and Camberwell and Peckham Times,* 10 December 1904.

26. "Faith Dancers," *London Daily Chronicle,* 5 December 1904; "Holy Jiggery"; "Holy Dancers Hotly Assailed," *Morning Leader* (London), 7 December 1904.

27. "The Dancers," *Star* (London), 6 December 1904; "Needless Violence," *Daily Mirror* (London), 9 December 1904.

28. "Dancing Delirium—Pentecostal Scenes at Camberwall—Four Hours of Acrobatic Revivalism," [1904], Hannah Whitall Smith Papers, File "Pentecostal Dancers," Asbury Theological Seminary Archives, Asbury, Kentucky.

29. White, *Story* (1935–43), 2:364.

30. Arthur C. Bray, "Impressions of London," *Rocky Mountain Pillar of Fire,* 15 February 1905, 5.

31. Alma White, "Mrs. White's London Letter," *Rocky Mountain Pillar of Fire,* 15 February 1905, 4–5.

32. Ibid., 4.

33. "Pentecostal Dancers at Dowlais," photocopy without name of newspaper, n.d.

34. Reconstructing the story is difficult because information is available only from the Pillar of Fire and Burning Bush leaders who were engaged in a bitter polemic, each justifying their position. The following account is an attempt to untangle the facts from the fiction in the charges and counter-charges.

35. "Exposure of the Burning Bush," *The Burning Bush Exposed* (Denver: Pillar of Fire, December 1905), 6–7. See also White, *Story* (1935–43), 2:383.

36. *The Burning Bush Exposed No. 2* (Denver: The Pillar of Fire, 1906), 3.

37. *Burning Bush,* 18 January 1906, 2.

38. Ibid., 3.

39. *Burning Bush,* 15 February 1906, 6.

40. Caroline Garretson, "Mrs. Garretson's Statement," *Burning Bush Exposed, No. 2,* 2.

41. "Exposure of the Burning Bush," 10.

42. Ibid., 11; White, *Story* (1935–43), 2:369.

43. *Burning Bush,* 18 January 1906, 7.

44. "Exposure of the Burning Bush," 12.

45. These are representative of the many groups, individuals, and magazines lambasted in the pages of the *Burning Bush* during 1905.

46. Godbey, *Autobiography,* 150–51. For two examples of attacks on Godbey, see the *Burning Bush,* 30 November 1905, 5; and 1 March 1906, 4.

47. White, *Story* (1935–43), 2:389.

48. C. W. Bridwell, "Recent Trip of the Burning Bush Leaders to Denver," *Burning Bush Exposed,* 19.

49. White, *Story* (1935–43), 2:393.

50. C. W. Bridwell, "Recent Trip of the Burning Bush Leaders to Denver," 19.

51. Mary Brassfield, "Hearing from Heaven," *Burning Bush Exposed,* 29.

52. Ibid., 30.

53. "Workers Resign from Burning Bush in Los Angeles," *Burning Bush Exposed No. 2,* 19–20.

54. Mary Brassfield, "Los Angeles Saints Get Their Bearings," *Burning Bush Exposed No. 2,* 20–21.

55. "Moore and Ingler's Resignation," *Burning Bush Exposed No. 2,* 18–19. Timothy L. Smith mentioned Ingler in his history of the Church of the Nazarene. Ingler was a gospel singer who had been affiliated with the Association of Pentecostal Churches in New England, a group that merged with others to become what is now call the Church of the Nazarene. Timothy L. Smith, *Called unto Holiness: The Formative Years* (Kansas City, Mo.: Nazarene Publishing House, 1962), 128.

56. *Burning Bush,* 25 January 1906, 6.

57. Correspondence from John and Sarah Johnson to Kent and Alma White, August and November 1906.

58. White, *Story* (1935–43), 2:394.

59. *Rocky Mountain Pillar of Fire,* 15 February 1905, 10.

60. White, *Story* (1935–43), 3:66.

61. "Woman Bishop Keeps 'Pillar of Fire' Burning," *Salisbury Evening Post*

(North Carolina), 27 August 1937, in Paige and Ingler, *Alma White's Evangelism,* 2:209.

62. Benton Johnson mentions tension in his sociological analysis of church and sect. Benton Johnson, "On Church and Sect," *American Sociological Review* 28 (August 1963): 544. William Bainbridge and Rodney Stark stress the element of tension in Johnson's definition, claiming that sects experience high tension with their environment, whereas churches have low tension or none. William Sims Bainbridge and Rodney Stark, "Sectarian Tension," *Review of Religious Research* 22, no. 2 (December 1980): 105.

63. White, *Looking Back From Beulah,* 358.

64. White, *Story* (1935–43), 3:14.

65. "'Jumpers' of Denver," *Washington Post,* 25 August 1907.

66. *Guide to Holiness,* February 1875, quoted in Richard Wheatley, *The Life and Letters of Mrs. Phoebe Palmer* (New York: W. C. Palmer, 1881; reprint, New York: Garland Publishing, 1984), 605–6.

67. Charles E. Jones, *Perfectionist Persuasion: The Holiness Movement and American Methodism, 1867–1936,* ATLA Monograph Series, no. 5 (Metuchen, N.J.: Scarecrow Press, 1974), 10.

68. "'Jumpers' of Denver," *Washington Post,* 25 August 1907.

69. "A Jersey Bishop on Her Travels," *Newark News* (New Jersey), 9 April 1926, in Paige and Ingler, *Alma White's Evangelism,* 2:73–74.

70. Helen Swarth, *My Life in a Commune* (N.p., n.d.), 70, 17.

71. Ibid., 30.

72. Arthur K. White, *Some More White Family History* (Denver: Pillar of Fire, 1980), 119.

73. Alice Freedland Diary, 7 October 1907, 15 October 1907 and 23 November 1907.

74. Della Huffman Diary, handwritten, 29 January 1908.

75. Jennie Fowler Willing, "God's Great Women: God's Modern Woman," *Guide to Holiness,* December 1897, 226.

76. Ronald L. Numbers, *Prophetess of Health: A Study of Ellen G. White* (New York: Harper & Row, 1976), 81, 82, 199.

77. White, *Story* (1935–43), 3:371.

78. Alma White, *Why I Do not Eat Meat* (Zarephath, N.J.: Pillar of Fire, 1938) 73.

79. Ibid., 37.

80. Numbers, *Prophetess of Health,* 54, 161.

81. White, *Why I Do not Eat Meat,* 116–20.

82. White, *Story* (1935–43), 4:50–51.

83. White, *Why I Do not Eat Meat,* 188.

84. John W. V. Smith, *The Quest for Holiness and Unity* (Anderson, Ind.: Warner Press, 1980), 65.

85. Della Huffman, Diary, 27 December 1908.

86. White, *Story* (1935–43), 3:109, 110, 109.

87. Alma White, *Demons and Tongues* (Bound Brook, N.J.: Pentecostal Union, 1910; reprint, Zarephath, N.J.: Pillar of Fire, 1936) 67.

88. Amanda Berry Smith, *An Autobiography. The Story of the Lord's Dealings*

with Mrs. Amanda Smith the Colored Evangelist (Chicago: Meyer & Brother, 1893), 423.

89. Julia A. J. Foot, *A Brand Plucked from the Fire: An Autobiographical Sketch* (Cleveland: Privately published, 1879), 5–6. The statement was made by Thomas K. Doty in the introduction.

90. White, *Story* (1935–43), 3:123.

91. Ibid., 3:145.

92. Ibid., 3:125.

93. For example, see "Denver Woman Who Is Creating Sensation in East," *Denver Times*, 29 December 1902.

94. John L. Cowan, "Acrobatic Religionists: The Fantastic Faith of the Holy Jumpers—Some Account of the Origin, Growth, and Odd Practices of a Curious Western Cult," *Great Southwest Magazine*, June 1907, 67.

95. White, *Woman's Ministry*, 15–16. Ten years after leaving Alma, Kent denounced equality within marriage, claiming that "God's order" required submission of the wife to her husband. He also wrote that a woman could not serve as a pastor. This reflected a change of mind since participating in Alma's ordination service. Kent White, *The Word of God Coming Again: Return of Apostolic Faith Church and Works now Due* (Winton, Bournemouth, England: Apostolic Faith Church, 1919), 152–53, 157.

96. White, *Story* (1935–43), 3:144.

97. Kent White, "Victory Through Prevailing Prayer," (N.p., n.d.), 6.

98. White, *Story* (1935–43), 3:146.

99. White, *Heart and Husband*, 63-64; White, *Story* (1935–43), 3:148.

100. Ibid., 3:157.

101. Ibid., 3:165.

102. White, *Demons and Tongues*, 117, 87, 43.

103. White, *Story* (1935–43), 3:21; White, *Demons and Tongues*, 82.

104. White, *Demons and Tongues*, 67–68.

105. For an analysis of the holiness roots of pentecostalism, see Vincent Synan, *Holiness-Pentecostal Movement*, chaps. 1–4 and Donald W. Dayton, *Theological Roots of Pentecostalism* (Grand Rapids, Mich.: Francis Asbury Press of Zondervan Publishing House, 1987).

106. White, *Story* (1935–43), 3:21.

107. Alma White, *What I Saw in a Tongues' Meeting* (Denver: N.p., n.d.), n.p.

108. Alma White, "The Bridegroom of My Soul," 23 May 1910, handwritten copy.

109. White, "Victory Through Prevailing Prayer," 9.

110. Ibid., 10.

111. Ibid., 16.

112. White, *Story* (1935–43), 3:213.

113. Ibid., 3:262.

114. White, *Story* (1935–43), 3:376–78.

115. Cowan, "Acrobatic Religionists," 67.

116. Arthur K. White, *Some White Family History* (Denver: Pillar of Fire, 1948), 391.

117. White, *Story* (1935–43), 4:207, 250.

118. Godbey was readmitted to the Methodist Episcopal Church, South in 1918. He died two years later on September 12, 1920. *Journal Kentucky Conference Methodist Episcopal Church, South, 1921,* 72–73.

119. White, *Story* (1935–43), 4:251, 388.

120. Gertrude Metlen Wolfram, *The Widow of Zarephath,* 210.

121. White, *New Testament Church,* 325.

122. Evan Jerry Lawrence, "Alma White College: A History of Its Relationship to the Development of the Pillar of Fire" (Ed.D. diss., Columbia University, 1966), 39. Jerry Lawrence married Alma White's granddaughter, Arlene White.

123. Letter from Kent White to Alma White, dated 14 June 1915, quoted in Alma White, *My Heart and My Husband* (Zarephath, N.J.: Pillar of Fire, 1923), 81.

124. Letter from Kent White to Charles and Lillian Bridwell, 24 June 1918.

125. More liberal than many of her contemporaries, Alma also allowed divorce for personal safety or legal protection. White, *New Testament Church,* 193.

126. Catharine Brody, "Pastor-Husband Jealous Asserts Woman Bishop," *New York Globe,* 9 February 1921.

127. Letter from Kent White to Arthur White, 4 July 1938.

128. "Bishop Says Her Heart Is Broken," *World,* 1922.

129. White, *Story* (1935–43), 5:15.

130. "Pillar of Fire Head Examined at Trial," *Denver Rocky Mountain News,* 17 February 1922, 14.

131. Harmon Kallman, "Pillar of Fire Church History Linked to That of Founder's Family," *Denver Post,* 20 August 1955, 5.

CHAPTER 4

1. Alma White, "The Ku Klux Klan and Woman's Cause" (Zarephath, N.J.: Pillar of Fire, n.d.), 7.

2. Goldberg documents Klan donations to several churches in Colorado (*Hooded Empire: The Ku Klux Klan in Colorado* [Urbana: University of Illinois Press, 1981], 56, 59, 66, 67, 129).

3. Chalmers reported that in New Jersey robed Klan members attended Presbyterian, Baptist, and Methodist Episcopal churches. David M. Chalmers, *Hooded Americanism: The First Century of the Ku Klux Klan 1865–1965* (Garden City, N.Y.: Doubleday, 1965), 246.

4. "Ku Klux Klan Letter," *Denver Catholic Register,* 9 March 1922, 1.

5. White, *Story* (1935–43), 3:293. The *Good Citizen* was also an "effectual weapon against immorality and crime, the white slave traffic, the liquor curse, the oppression of women, cruelty to children, and other kindred evils so often overlooked by many of our good citizens" (3:293). Unfortunately, issues of *Good Citizen* were available only for years 1918 and 1919.

6. "*Denver Catholic Register* Historical Index 1913–1939" (N.p., n.d.).

7. "Self-Named Woman Bishop Violent in Anti-Catholicity," *Denver Catholic Register,* 1 February 1923, 1.

8. Chalmers, *Hooded Americanism,* 246; and Alma White, *Guardians of Liberty,* 3 vols. (Zarephath, N.J.: Pillar of Fire, 1943), 1:115. There are several discrepancies between the two reports of this meeting. Chalmers claimed it was "widely publicized" (p. 246). A. L. Wolfram, a Pillar of Fire member, claimed "no public advertising was done although some personal invitations and bills of advertising were given out" (1:114). Wolfram further indicated that the Pillar of Fire allowed the New Jersey Klan the use of their auditorium because it had the largest seating capacity in Bound Brook and did not suggest that the Klan was there to recruit Pillar of Fire members. Another source of information on this encounter is "12,000 of Klan out at Jersey Meeting," *New York Times,* 3 May 1923, 1.

9. White, *Guardians of Liberty,* 1:119–20.

10. Given the information at his disposal, it was impossible for Goldberg to determine how many Pillar of Fire members actually enlisted in the Ku Klux Klan. Robert Alan Goldberg, personal letter. Alma's endorsement of the Klan is an embarrassment to current Pillar of Fire members; every Pillar of Fire member interviewed by this author deplored her connection to the Klan.

11. White, *Story* (1935–43), 5:383.

12. Ibid., 5:214.

13. Hiram Evans Interview, Chicago, 1924, quoted in Charles W. Ferguson, *The Confusion of Tongues* (Garden City, N.Y.: Doubleday, Doran & Company, 1928), 269.

14. Chalmers, *Hooded Americanism,* 248. See also Goldberg, *Hooded Empire,* 7.

15. Ferenc Morton Szasz discusses the arguments relating to higher criticism and evolution in his book *The Divided Mind of Protestant America, 1880–1930* (University: University of Alabama Press, 1982).

16. "Ancestors Not the Tree-hanging Kind," *Colorado Springs Evening and Sunday Telegraph,* 20 July 1922, in Paige and Ingler, *Alma White's Evangelism,* 1:268–69.

17. White, *The New Testament Church,* 39.

18. For instance, at the Pillar of Fire conference in Cincinnati in 1925, evolution and modernism were the primary themes. "Pillar of Fire Conference to Discuss Evolution," *Cincinnati Commercial Tribune,* 22 June 1925, in Paige and Ingler, *Alma White's Evangelism,* 2:51.

19. Robert M. Miller, "A Note on the Relationship Between the Protestant Churches and the Revived Ku Klux Klan," *Journal of Southern History* 22 (August 1956): 363.

20. White, *Guardians of Liberty,* 1:78.

21. Michael Williams, *The Shadow of the Pope* (New York: McGraw Hill Book Company, 1932), 317. Denominational affiliations of nine clergy were unknown. Of the remaining seventeen, there were five Baptists, five Disciples, three Methodists, three Presbyterians, and one Episcopalian.

22. Ibid. Five each of the clergy officials were Methodists and Baptists,

two were Disciples, and one each was Presbyterian, Episcopalian, United Brethren, and Evangelical.

23. Goldberg, *Hooded Empire,* 113.

24. Ibid., 188.

25. Ibid., 18–19.

26. James H. Davis, "The Rise of the Ku Klux Klan in Colorado, 1921–1925" (Master's thesis, University of Denver, 1963), 46. Kenneth T. Jackson (*The Ku Klux Klan in the City: 1915–1930* [New York: Oxford University Press, 1967], 217) confirms the key role of these two congregations in supporting the Klan.

27. Chalmers, *Hooded Americanism,* 247, 293.

28. William G. McLoughlin, *Revivals, Awakenings, and Reform: An Essay on Religion and Social Change in America, 1607–1977,* Chicago History of American Religion (Chicago: University of Chicago Press, 1978), 149.

29. *Denver Post,* 18 June 1922, quoted in Goldberg, *Hooded Empire,* 16–17.

30. Ferguson, *Confusion of Tongues,* 253–54.

31. Chalmers (*Hooded Americanism,* 291) suggests the three million figure, whereas Goldberg (*Hooded Empire,* vii) offers the higher number.

32. Goldberg, *Hooded Empire,* 168, 164.

33. Kathleen M. Blee, *Women of the Klan* (Berkeley and Los Angeles: University of California Press, 1991), 172.

34. White, *Guardians of Liberty,* 1:81.

35. Alma White, *The Ku Klux Klan in Prophecy* (Zarephath, N.J.: The Good Citizen, 1925); Alma White, *Klansmen: Guardians of Liberty* (Zarephath, N.J.: The Good Citizen, 1926); and Alma White, *Heroes of the Fiery Cross* (Zarephath, N.J.: The Good Citizen, 1928). Seven chapters from *The Ku Klux Klan in Prophecy* and one from *Heroes of the Fiery Cross* are reprinted in volume 1 of *Guardians of Liberty.* Volume 2 of *Guardians of Liberty* consists of fifteen chapters, thirteen from *Klansmen: Guardians of Liberty* and one from *The Ku Klux Klan in Prophecy.* Five chapters in volume 3 of *Guardians of Liberty* first appeared in *Heroes of the Fiery Cross.* In the reprint editions, synonyms such as *patriots* and *the order* replaced explicit references to the Ku Klux Klan.

36. Papal statements fueled Alma's fears. For instance, Pope Leo XIII, in his encyclical "Christian Democracy" (1901), attacked popular sovereignty; government by consent of the governed; and freedom of religion, speech, assembly, and the press. Winthrop Hudson, *Religion in America,* 4th ed. (New York: Macmillan, 1987), 367.

37. White, *Story* (1935–43), 5:265.

38. White, *Heroes of Fiery Cross,* 140, 142. Alma deleted this portion of the lecture in the version printed in *Guardians of Liberty,* vol. 3.

39. Blee, *Women of the Klan,* 75–76, 197, referring to White, *Ku Klux Klan,* 53–54; White, *Heroes of Fiery Cross,* 33–34, 36; and Alma White, *Woman's Chains* (Zarephath, N.J.: Pillar of Fire, 1943), 49–59. In the pages cited from *Woman's Chains,* Alma made no references to Jews.

40. See Timothy P. Weber, *Living in the Shadow of the Second Coming* (New York: Oxford University Press, 1979), 128–57, for a summary of premillennialist support for Jews, which grew out of the belief that the restoration of

Israel and the Second Coming of Christ were related.

41. Alma White, *Jerusalem, Egypt, Palestine, Syria* (Zarephath, N.J.: Pillar of Fire, 1936, 1944), 147. See also Alma White, *The Restoration of Israel: The Hope of the World* (Zarephath, N.J.: The Pentecostal Union [Pillar of Fire], 1917), 128.

42. Ibid., 85.

43. David S. Wyman, *Paper Walls: America and the Refugee Crisis 1938–1941* (Amherst: University of Massachusetts Press, 1968), 27–28.

44. "Pillar of Fire Revival Ends," *Somerville Gazette* (New Jersey), 29 August 1933, in Paige and Ingler, *Alma White's Evangelism*, 2:137.

45. George E. Gooderham, "The Pillar of Fire. 1934," in *Denver Cults: 1934–1937*, ed. William Henry Bernhardt (Denver: N.p., 1937), 163.

46. David S. Wyman, *The Abandonment of the Jews: America and the Holocaust, 1941–1945* (New York: Pantheon Books, 1984).

47. White, *Story* (1935–43), 2:258.

48. Ibid., 5:236. See also 5:270 and White, *Guardians of Liberty*, 1:56.

49. White, *Guardians of Liberty*, 2:43.

50. Ibid., 1:15, 52.

51. See Adam W. Miller, *An Introduction to the New Testament* (Anderson, Ind.: Warner Press, 1946), 333–39, for a summary of the church-historical interpretation of Revelation.

52. Godbey, *Autobiography*, 169.

53. White, *Guardians of Liberty*, 1:28, 2:12.

54. Ibid., 2:40.

55. John Higham, *Strangers in the Land: Patterns of American Nativism, 1860–1925* (New York: Atheneum, 1963), 178–79.

56. For a brief summary of anti-Catholic feeling prior to the Civil War, see Sydney E. Ahlstrom, *A Religious History of the American People* (New Haven: Yale University Press, 1972), 558–68. The Know-Nothings, officially the American party, mobilized anti-Catholic feeling in the 1850s as the Ku Klux Klan did in the 1920s.

57. White, *Story* (1935–43), 3:216.

58. *New Brunswick Daily Home News*, quoted in White, *Guardians of Liberty*, 1:119.

59. White, *Guardians of Liberty*, 2:8; and Alma White, "Ahasuerus, the Despot," in *Radio Sermons*, 181.

60. White, *New Testament Church*, 317; and White, *Guardians of Liberty*, 1:95.

61. White, *Guardians of Liberty*, 1:42–43.

62. Ibid., 1:90.

63. Ibid., 2:22, 16.

64. Department of Justice, Immigration and Naturalization Service, *Annual Reports*, quoted in Ahlstrom, *Religious History*, 749–50.

65. Ibid., 562.

66. White, *Story* (1935–43), 5:iv. Arthur White wrote the introduction to this volume.

67. White, *Guardians of Liberty*, 2:99.

68. White, "James Monroe," in *Radio Sermons,* 288.

69. Charlotte Perkins Gilman, "Let Sleeping Forefathers Lie," *Forerunner* 6 (October 1915): 263, quoted in Mary A. Hill, *Charlotte Perkins Gilman: The Making of a Radical Feminist, 1860–1926* (Philadelphia: Temple University Press, 1980), 279.

70. Aileen S. Kraditor, ed., *Up from the Pedestal: Selected Writings in the History of American Feminism* (Chicago: Quadrangle Books, 1968), 257–59.

71. White, "James Monroe," 288.

72. White, *Story* (1935–43), 5:320. Lenwood G. Davis and Janet L. Sims-Wood, comp., *The Ku Klux Klan: A Bibliography* (Westport, Conn.: Greenwood Press, 1984), 629.

73. White, *Guardians of Liberty,* 3:100.

74. It was not until 1896 that more "new" than "old" immigrants entered the United States. Maldwyn Allen Jones, *American Immigration* (Chicago: University of Chicago Press, 1960), 179. Jones dispels the traditional interpretation of the dichotomy of "old" and "new" immigrants fostered by the report of the Dillingham Commission (pp. 177–81).

75. Ibid., 258–59, 267. Jones summarizes restriction demands between 1882 and 1924 (pp. 247–77).

76. Dorothy M. Brown, *Setting a Course: American Women in the 1920s* (Boston: Twayne Publishers, 1987), 20.

77. See James J. Kenneally, "Eve, Mary and the Historians: American Catholicism and Women," *Horizons* 3 (1976): 189–90, 200.

78. *Good Citizen,* January 1919, cover.

79. Arthur K. White, "A Dogma of the Medieval Church that Makes for Female Oppression," *Woman's Chains,* May–June 1924, 6.

80. Higham, *Strangers in the Land,* 179.

81. Alma White, "Opposition of the Clergy to Women's Ministry," *Woman's Chains,* January–February 1924, 4.

82. White, *Ku Klux Klan in Prophecy,* 136. This statement was from an address entitled "The Ku Klux Klan and Women's Cause" delivered in Brooklyn, 31 December 1922, during the Pillar of Fire Annual Jubilee services.

83. Davis and Sims-Wood, *Ku Klux Klan,* 629.

84. White, *Ku Klux Klan in Prophecy,* 130.

85. Goldberg, *Hooded Empire,* 89.

86. Sheila M. Rothman, *Woman's Proper Place: A History of Changing Ideals and Practices, 1870 to the Present* (New York: Basic Books, 1978), 81–83, 196–97.

87. For a discussion of voluntary motherhood and suffragists' opposition to contraception, see Linda Gordon, "Voluntary Motherhood: The Beginnings of Feminist Birth Control Ideas in the United States," in *Clio's Consciousness Raised: New Perspectives on the History of Women,* ed. Mary S. Hartman and Lois Banner (New York: Octagon Books, 1976), 54–71.

88. Blee, *Women of the Klan,* 49.

89. Goldberg, *Hooded Empire,* 89.

90. Sarah M. Grimké, *Letters on the Equality of the Sexes and the Condition of*

Woman (Boston: Isaac Knapp, 1838; reprint, New York: Source Book Press, 1970), 60.

91. *History of Woman Suffrage*, vols. 1–3, ed. Elizabeth Cady Stanton, Susan B. Anthony, and Matilda Joslyn Gage (Rochester, N.Y.: Charles Mann, 1881, 1882, 1885). Vol. 4 ed. Susan B. Anthony and Ida Husted Harper (Indianapolis: Hollenbeck Press, 1902). Vols. 5 and 6 ed. Ida Husted Harper (New York: J. J. Little & Ives, 1922), 1:72.

92. Ibid., 5:222.

93. White, *Woman's Ministry*, 5.

94. Alma White, "The Chains of Women," *Woman's Chains*, March–April 1924, 4.

95. Alma White, "The Chains of Women," *Woman's Chains*, March–April 1928, 3.

96. Frances Willard, letter in *War Cry*, 5 May 1894, p. 3, quoted in Norris Magnuson, *Salvation in the Slums*, ATLA Series, no. 10 (Metuchen, N.J.: Scarecrow Press, 1977), 115.

97. See White, *Beauty of Holiness*, particularly chapter 7, "Phoebe Palmer as Feminist." Harold Raser, another biographer speaks of her "sanctified feminism" in which she limited women's equality to the work of evangelism. However, he does recognize that her views, particularly those expressed in *Promise of the Father*, offered potential for expanding women's role in church and society. Raser, *Phoebe Palmer*, 208–10.

98. Wesleyan/Holiness women frequently spoke of the empowerment of the Holy Spirit that enabled them to preach. For a discussion of this theme, see Susie C. Stanley, "Empowered Foremothers: Wesleyan/Holiness Women Speak to Today's Christian Feminists," *Wesleyan Theological Journal*, 1989:103–16.

99. Roberts, *Ordaining Women*. With the exception of Alma White, Roberts's book provided the most thorough expression of women's equality from a Wesleyan/Holiness perspective.

100. Jennie Fowler Willing, "Every Woman a Missionary," *Guide to Holiness*, November 1896, 178.

101. White, *Story* (1935–43), 2:85.

102. Grimké, *Letters on Equality*, 4.

103. *History of Woman Suffrage*, 1:103.

104. Ibid., 1:80.

105. L. S. Lawrence, "Prejudice Against Women," *Woman's Chains*, March–April 1925, 8.

106. Lee Anna Starr, *The Bible Status of Woman* (N.p., 1926, reprint, Zarephath, N.J.: Pillar of Fire, 1955). Advertisements promoting the book appeared frequently in *Woman's Chains*.

107. Arthur K. White, "The Bible Status of Women," *Woman's Chains*, July–August 1927, 4–6; Arthur K. White, "Attitude of Jesus in 'The Bible Status of Women,'" *Woman's Chains*, September–October 1927, 4–6; and Arthur K. White, "The Pauline and Hierarchical Attitudes in 'The Bible Status of Women,'" *Woman's Chains*, November–December 1927, 4–6.

108. *History of Woman Suffrage*, 3:322.

109. For example, see White, "Woman's Place," 204, and White, *Story* (1935–43), 5:125–26.

110. White, "Opposition of the Clergy," 5.

111. Grant Cross, "Women's Emancipation in Order," *Woman's Chains,* January–February 1928, 14.

112. *Catechism of the Pillar of Fire Church* (Denver: Pillar of Fire, 1948), 19.

113. For an example, see Rev. A. H. Strong's argument as quoted in Matilda Joslyn Gage, *Woman, Church and State: The Original Expose of Male Collaboration against the Female Sex* (New York: Truth Seeker Company, 1893; reprint, Watertown, Mass.: Persephone Press, 1980), 210. Strong was president of Rochester Theological Seminary.

114. Roberts, *Ordaining Women,* 49; Cross, "Woman's Emancipation in Order," 14.

115. For a representative example, see "May Women Preach?" *Quarterly Review of the Methodist Episcopal Church, South,* n.s. 3 (July 1881): 482.

116. Grimké, *Letters on Equality,* 7; Wilson, *Scripture View,* 26; and Jennie Fowler Willing, "God's Great Women: Eve," *Guide to Holiness,* January 1897, 29.

117. White, "Woman's Chains," 3; and Roberts, *Ordaining Women,* 10.

118. Cross, "Woman's Emancipation in Order," 14–15.

119. White, *Story* (1935–43), 5:132.

120. L. S. Lawrence, "Was St. Paul Opposed to Women Preachers?" *Woman's Chains,* July–August 1948, 7; Arthur K. White, *Crusading Christian Women* (Zarephath, N.J.: Pillar of Fire, 1963), 187.

121. White, *Story* (1935–43), 5:304. Jennie Fowler Willing, *The Open Door,* October 1910, 15, quoted in Joanne Elizabeth C. Brown, "Jennie Fowler Willing (1834–1916): Methodist Churchwoman and Reformer" (Ph.D. diss., Boston University Graduate School, 1983), 187.

122. White, *Woman's Chains,* 77.

123. Carolyn Field Staats, "The High Calling of Women," *Woman's Chains,* January–February 1928, 13.

124. Alma White, "When Will Woman's Freedom Be Completed?" *Woman's Chains,* January–February 1946, 6; Alma White, "Inequality Between the Sexes, *Woman's Chains,* November–December 1938, 6.

125. Roberts, *Ordaining Women,* 58.

126. *History of Woman Suffrage,* 2:399.

127. Religious convictions should not be discounted entirely, however, because no one has explored the religious motivations of National Woman's Party members. Intriguingly, the Schlesinger Library's copy of Elizabeth Wilson's *A Scriptural View of Woman's Rights and Duties* was previously owned by Inez Haynes Irwin, a prominent National Woman's Party member and historian of the organization.

128. White, "Woman's Place," 207.

129. "Who Are the Pillar of Fire?" *New Brunswick Times* (N.J.), 25 June 1916, in Paige and Ingler, *Alma White's Evangelism,* 1:13.

130. Ida C. Turner, "Woman," *Good Citizen,* September 1919, 10–11.

131. "News Items," *Good Citizen,* July 1918, 10; and "Suffrage in Doubt,"

Good Citizen, November 1919, 12. Unfortunately, the only copies of *Good Citizen* available were for the years 1918 and 1919.

132. *History of Woman Suffrage,* 3:230.

133. Magnuson, *Salvation in the Slums,* 244.

134. *Christian Herald,* 26 July 1916, 876, and 23 January 1918, 109, quoted in Magnuson, *Salvation in the Slums,* 117.

135. White, *Story* (1935–43), 5:314 and 4:237. See also 4:369.

136. *New York Times,* 11 September 1920, quoted in Marjory Nelson, "Ladies in the Streets: A Sociological Analysis of the National Woman's Party" (Ph.D. diss., State University of New York at Buffalo, 1976), 150.

137. White, *Story* (1935–43), 5:108.

138. "Door of Opportunity Opens for Women," *Somerville Unionist Gazette* (N.J.), 16 December 1920, in Paige and Ingler, *Alma White's Evangelism,* 1:166.

139. To give just two examples, Alma preached this sermon at Jacksonville, Florida on 29 May 1921 and at Denver in March 1922. White, *Story* (1935–43), 5:54, 108.

140. "The Handwriting on the Wall," *State Center-Record,* Bound Brook, N.J., 23 June 1922, in Paige and Ingler, *Alma White's Evangelism,* 1:257.

141. White, *Story* (1935–43), 5:229, 246, 346.

142. "Door of Opportunity Opens for Women," in Paige and Ingler, *Alma White's Evangelism,* 1:164.

143. White, "The Chains of Women" (1928), 4.

144. Alma White, "Shall Woman Occupy Her Place?" *Woman's Chains,* January–February 1926, 5.

145. *Woman's Chains,* November–December 1927, 8, and *Woman's Chains,* July–August 1932, 5.

146. Kathleen White, "My Story of the Republican Convention," *Woman's Chains,* July–August 1940, 13.

147. Inez Garretson, "True Home-Maker," *Woman's Chains,* January–February 1925, 8.

148. G. W. [Gertrude Wolfram], "Woman for the United States Senate," *Woman's Chains,* March–April 1928, 16.

149. "Inactivity in Voting Deplored," *New York Evening Journal,* 27 December 1923, in Paige and Ingler, *Alma White's Evangelism,* 1:305.

150. "Woman Bishop Opens Revival—Topic: 'Woman's Chains,'" *Brooklyn Daily Times,* 27 December 1923, in Paige and Ingler, *Alma White's Evangelism,* 1:307.

151. Gertrude Wolfram, "What Can Women Do?" *Woman's Chains,* September–October 1924, 9. Gertrude Wolfram's husband recommended that women should fill their share of governmental offices. A. L. Wolfram, "Women and Men Must Unite Their Efforts," *Woman's Chains,* March–April 1924, 8.

152. Gilbert Haven shared Alma's vision. *History of Woman Suffrage,* 3:529; "Scaling the Heights," *Woman's Chains,* July–August 1925, 7.

153. Alma White, "Equality Equal to Success," *Woman's Chains,* July–August 1924, 4.

154. White, *Story* (1935–43), 5:198.

155. Inez Haynes Irwin, "The Equal Rights Amendment: Why the Woman's Party is for It," *Good Housekeeping,* March 1924, 18.

156. Edna Kenton, "The Ladies' Next Step: The Case for the Equal Rights Amendment," *Harper's Magazine,* February 1926, 372.

157. *Equal Rights,* 3 January 1925, 272.

158. L. S. L. [L. S. Lawrence], "Should We Have an ERA?" *Woman's Chains,* May–June 1924, 15.

159. Alma White, "Equality Essential to Success," *Woman's Chains,* July–August 1924, 3. The article title reflects the centrality of equality in Alma's thought.

160. White, *Story* (1935–43), 3:237–38.

161. Two scholars who advance the consensus viewpoint are J. Stanley Lemons, *Woman Citizen: Social Feminism in the 1920s* (Urbana: University of Illinois Press, 1973), 182 and Susan Ware, *Holding Their Own: American Women in the 1930s* (Boston: Twayne Publishers, 1982), 109.

162. Quoted in White, *Story* (1935–43), 5:329.

163. According to National Woman's Party records, which are incomplete, Alma was not a member of the National Woman's Party. Sharon Griffith, Executive Director, National Woman's Party, letter to author, 14 May 1984.

164. *Woman's Chains,* March–April 1926, 7.

165. Leila Enders, "What the National Woman's Party Has Done for Women in New Jersey 1925–1928," *Woman's Chains,* July–August 1928, 13–14. Enders was the chairperson of the New Jersey branch of the National Woman's Party.

166. "Current Events," *Woman's Chains,* March–April 1924, 14. Mary DuBrow taught in New Jersey before joining the National Woman's Party suffrage campaign in 1918 as an organizer and speaker. She participated in the watchfire demonstrations sponsored by the National Woman's Party in January 1919 and was sentenced to ten days in jail for her part in the nonviolent protest of President Wilson's nonsupport of woman suffrage. Doris Stevens, *Jailed for Freedom: The Story of the Militant American Suffrage Movement* (New York: Boni & Liveright, 1920; reprint, New York: Schocken Books, 1976), 358.

167. Lemons, *Woman Citizen,* 57.

168. Susan Ware, *Beyond Suffrage: Women in the New Deal* (Cambridge: Harvard University Press, 1981), 79. Ware noted that two of the twenty-eight women in the network supported the ERA.

169. Florence Kelley, "Shall Women Be Equal Before the Law?" *Nation* 12 April 1922, 421, quoted in Rothman, *Woman's Proper Place,* 160.

170. J. Stanley Lemons accepts the social reformers' propaganda that the National Woman's Party supported the ERA for selfish motives. Lemons, *Woman Citizen,* 48, 205. The National Woman's Party, however, claimed to have working women's interests at heart. See Harriot Stanton Blatch, *Challenging Years: The Memoirs of Harriot Stanton Blatch* (New York: G. P. Putnam's Sons, 1940), 289, 322 and Alma Lutz, "Shall Women's Work be Regulated

by Law?" *Atlantic Monthly,* September 1930, 323.

171. Alma White, "Woman's Ministry—The Teaching of the Bible," *Woman's Chains,* January–February 1932, 6.

172. Kathleen M. White, "A New Amendment to the Constitution," *Woman's Chains,* January–February 1944, 12.

173. Harriet McCormick, interview with author, Denver, Colorado, 14 December 1981.

174. White, *Story* (1935–43), 4:243.

175. *Dry Legion* ceased publication in 1970.

176. "Bishop vs. Drink," *Time,* 18 December 1939, 40; and "Pillar of Fire Dry Legion Acts Our Evils of Liquor in Brooklyn Church Pulpit," *Life,* 29 January 1940, 42–43.

177. Alma White Diary, 14 March 1940.

178. Alma White Diary, 6 November 1934.

179. Letter quoted in Arlene White Lawrence, "Radio Birthdays, East and West; Pillar of Fire Celebrates KPOF 50th Anniversary," *Pillar of Fire,* 15 April 1978, 6–7.

180. After Alma's death, the Pillar of Fire expanded its radio ministry with the purchase of two other radio stations, WAWZ-FM in Zarephath (1954) and WAKW-AM in Cincinnati (1961). As of 1992, three stations remained in operation: KPOF-AM, WAWZ-FM and WAKW-AM.

181. White, *Story* (1935–43), 5:186.

182. "Pillar," *American Magazine,* May 1937, 101. "Fundamentalist Pillar," *Time,* 8 July 1946, 73.

183. White, *Some White Family History,* 391.

184. "Pillar of Fire Properties," typed list.

185. Evan Jerry Lawrence, "Alma White College: A History of Its Relationship to the Development of the Pillar of Fire" (Ed.D. diss., Columbia University, 1966), 113.

186. National Council of Church of Christ, *Yearbook of American Churches.* The 5,100 membership figure was repeated in the yearbook until 1967 after which time no statistics have been provided.

187. Alma White Diary, 5 December 1929.

188. Alma White Diary, 22 December 1940.

189. Alma White Diary, 8 July 1929.

190. Alma White Diary, 6 January 1937. Ray had married Grace E. Miller in 1916. They had no children. Alma White Diary, 2 December 1937.

191. Alma White Diary, 19, 20 December 1933.

192. Letter from Kent White to Alma White, 20 March 1916, quoted in White, *My Heart and My Husband,* 88.

193. Letter from Kent White to Arthur White, 4 July 1938.

194. Alma White Diary, 18 July 1940.

195. White, *Some White Family History,* 408.

196. "Woman Bishop Keeps 'Pillar of Fire' Burning," *Salisbury Evening Post* (North Carolina), 27 August 1937, in Paige and Ingler, *Alma White's Evangelism,* 2:208.

197. "Alma White Centennial 1862–1962" (N.p., n.d.).

EPILOG

1. White, *Crusading Christian Women*, 170.
2. Alma White, "Equality Essential to Moral, Political & Spiritual Progress," *Woman's Chains*, November–December 1944, 5.

Bibliography

PILLAR OF FIRE SOURCES

Books

Catechism of the Pillar of Fire Church. Denver: Pillar of Fire, 1948.

Paige, C. [Clara] R., and C. [Clifford] K. Ingler, eds. *Alma White's Evangelism: Press Reports*. 2 vols. Zarephath, N.J.: Pillar of Fire, 1939–40.

Starr, Lee Anna. *The Bible Status of Woman*. New York: Fleming H. Revell Co., 1926. Reprint. Zarephath, N.J.: Pillar of Fire, 1955.

White, Alma. *The Bugle Call: The Hymns and Songs of Alma White, with Other Favorite Selections*. Zarephath, N.J.: Pillar of Fire, 1943.

_____. *The Chosen People*. Zarephath, N.J.: Pillar of Fire, 1946.

_____. *Demons and Tongues*. Bound Brook, N.J.: Pentecostal Union, 1910. Reprint. Zarephath, N.J.: Pillar of Fire, 1936.

_____. *Everlasting Life*. Zarephath, N.J.: Pillar of Fire, 1944.

_____. *Gems of Life: Short Selections for Children*. Bound Brook, N.J.: Pillar of Fire Publishers, 1907.

_____. *Golden Sunbeams*. Zarephath, N.J.: Pillar of Fire, 1956.

_____. *Gospel Truth*. Zarephath, N.J.: Pillar of Fire, 1945.

_____. *Guardians of Liberty*. 3 vols. Zarephath, N.J.: Pillar of Fire, 1943.

_____. *Heroes of the Fiery Cross*. Zarephath, N.J.: Good Citizen, 1928.

_____. *Hymns and Poems*. Zarephath, N.J.: Pillar of Fire, 1946.

_____. *Jerusalem, Egypt, Palestine, Syria*. Zarephath, N.J.: Pillar of Fire, 1936.

_____. *Klansmen: Guardians of Liberty*. Zarephath, N.J.: Good Citizen, 1926.

_____. *The Ku Klux Klan in Prophecy*. Zarephath, N.J.: Good Citizen, 1925.

_____. *Looking Back from Beulah*. Denver: Pentecostal Union, 1902. Reprint. Zarephath, N.J.: Pillar of Fire, 1951.

_____. *Modern Miracles and Answers to Prayer*. Zarephath, N.J.: Pillar of Fire, 1939.

_____. *Musings of the Past*. Zarephath, N.J.: Pillar of Fire, 1927.

_____. *My Heart and My Husband*. Zarephath, N.J.: Pillar of Fire, 1923.

_____. *The New Testament Church*. Denver: Pillar of Fire, 1907. Rev. ed. Zarephath, N.J.: Pillar of Fire, 1929.

_____. *Radio Sermons and Lectures*. Denver: Pillar of Fire, 1936.

_____. *Restoration of Israel, the Hope of the World*. Zarephath, N.J.: Pentecostal Union, 1917.

_____. *Short Sermons*. Zarephath, N.J.: Pillar of Fire, 1932.

———. *The Story of My Life and the Pillar of Fire*, 6 vols. Zarephath, N.J.: Pillar of Fire, 1919–34.

———. *The Story of My Life and the Pillar of Fire*. 5 vols. Zarephath, N.J.: Pillar of Fire, 1935–43.

———. *The Sword of the Spirit*. Zarephath, N.J.: Pillar of Fire, 1937.

———. *The Titanic Tragedy—God Speaking to the Nations*. Bound Brook, N.J.: Pentecostal Union, 1912.

———. *Truth Stranger than Fiction*. Zarephath, N.J.: Pentecostal Union, 1913.

———. *The Voice of Nature*. Zarephath, N.J.: Pillar of Fire, 1927.

———. *Why I Do not Eat Meat*. Zarephath, N.J.: Pillar of Fire, 1939.

———. *With God in the Yellowstone*. Zarephath, N.J.: Pillar of Fire, 1920.

White, Alma, and Arthur K. White, eds. *Cross and Crown Hymnal*. Zarephath, N.J.: Pillar of Fire, 1939.

———. *The Harp of Gold* or *Pillar of Fire Praises No. 2*. Zarephath, N.J.: Pentecostal Union, 1911.

———. *The Silver Trumpet: Hymnal of the Church of the Pillar of Fire*. Zarephath, N.J.: Pillar of Fire, 1926.

———. *Woman's Chains*. Zarephath, N.J.: Pillar of Fire, 1943.

White, Arthur K. *Crusading Christian Women*. Zarephath, N.J.: Pillar of Fire, 1963.

———. *Some More White Family History*. Zarephath, N.J.: Pillar of Fire, 1980.

———. *Some White Family History*. Denver: Pillar of Fire, 1948.

White, Ray B. *Doctrines and Discipline of the Pillar of Fire Church*. Zarephath, N.J.: Pillar of Fire, 1918.

Wolfram, Gertrude Metlen. *The Widow of Zarephath: A Church in the Making*. Zarephath, N.J.: Pillar of Fire, 1954.

Articles and Pamphlets

Bray, Arthur C. "Impressions of London." *Rocky Mountain Pillar of Fire*, 14 February 1905, 5.

A Brief Account of the Religious, Educational and Benevolent Activities of the Pillar of Fire Movement. N.p., 1937.

The Burning Bush Exposed. Denver: Pillar of Fire, 1905.

The Burning Bush Exposed No.2. Denver: Pillar of Fire, 1906.

Good Citizen. 1918–19.

Lawrence, Arlene White. "Radio Birthdays, East and West; Pillar of Fire Celebrates KPOF 50th Anniversary." *Pillar of Fire*, 15 April 1978, 6–9.

Religious, Educational and Benevolent Activities of the Pillar of Fire Movement. N.p., 1941.

Religious, Educational and Benevolent Activities of the Pillar of Fire Movement. N.p., 1966.

What Smoking Does to Women. Zarephath, N. J.: Pillar of Fire, n.d.

White, Alma. "The Ku Klux Klan and Woman's Cause." Zarephath, N.J.: Pillar of Fire, n.d.

———. "Mrs. White's London Letter." *Rocky Mountain Pillar of Fire*, 15 February 1905, 4–5.

_____. *What I Saw in a Tongues' Meeting.* Denver: Pillar of Fire, n.d.

_____. *Woman's Ministry.* London: Pillar of Fire, [1921].

Woman's Chains. January–December 1924; January–June 1925, January–April 1926, July–December 1927, January–December 1928, January–April 1932, January–February 1937, November–December 1938, January–December 1940, January–June 1941, January–December 1944, January–February 1946, January–December 1948, November 1970.

Unpublished Materials

"Alma White Centennial 1862–1962." N.p., n.d.

Bridwell, Mollie, to Kent White, 10 November 1883; 28 November 1886.

Freedland, Alice. Diary, 1907.

Huffman, Della. Diary, 1908.

Johnson, John, and Sarah Johnson, to Kent White and Alma White, August and November 1906.

Lawrence, Arlene White. Interviews with author, 1981–91, Denver and Zarephath, N.J.

Lawrence, Evan Jerry. "Alma White College: A History of Its Relationship to the Development of the Pillar of Fire." Ph.D. diss., Columbia University, 1966.

McCormick, Harriet. Interview with author, 14 December 1981, Denver.

Pearsall, James. Interviews with author, 1986–92, Zarephath, N.J.

"Pillar of Fire Properties." Typed list.

Staats, Carolyn. Interview with author, 14 December 1981, Denver.

White, Alma. "The Bridegroom of My Soul," 23 May 1910. Handwritten copy.

_____. "Commencement Address." Zarephath, N. J., 11 June 1935.

_____. Diary. 1927–31, 1933–37, 1939, 1940–41, 1944–46.

White, Kent. "Early Important Dates in My Life." N.d.

White, Kent, to Alma White, 14 June 1915.

White, Kent, to Arthur White, 4 July 1938.

White, Kent, to Charles and Lillian Bridwell, 24 June 1918.

White, Kent, to Mollie Bridwell, 20 November 1886; and 8 April 1887.

OTHER PRIMARY SOURCES

Books

Beardsley, Isaac Haight. *Echoes from Peak and Plain; or Tales of Life, War, Travel and Colorado Methodism.* Cincinnati: Curts & Jennings, 1898.

Bilhartz, Terry D., comp. and ed. *Francis Asbury's America: An Album of Early American Methodism.* Grand Rapids, Mich.: Francis Asbury Press of Zondervan Publishing House, 1984.

Blatch, Harriot Stanton, and Alma Lutz. *Challenging Years: The Memoirs of Harriot Stanton Blatch.* New York: G. P. Putnam's Sons, 1940.

Clarke, Adam. *The Holy Bible . . . with a Commentary and Critical Notes.* 6 vols. New York: Abingdon, n.d.

Cook, Sarah A. *The Handmaiden of the Lord, or Wayside Sketches.* Chicago: T. B. Arnold, 1896.

Foote, Julia A. J. *A Brand Plucked from the Fire.* Cleveland: Privately published, 1879.

Gage, Matilda Joslyn. *Woman, Church and State: The Original Exposé of Male Collaboration against the Female Sex.* New York: Truth Seeker, 1893. Reprint. Watertown, Mass.: Persephone Press, 1980.

Godbey, William B. *Autobiography of Rev. W. B. Godbey, A.m.* Cincinnati: God's Revivalist Office, 1909.

_____. *Victory.* Cincinnati: M. W. Knapp, 1888.

Grimké, Sarah M. *Letters on the Equality of the Sexes and the Condition of Woman.* Boston: Isaac Knapp, 1838. Reprint. New York: Source Book Press, 1970.

History of Woman Suffrage. Vol. 1–3 ed. Elizabeth Cady Stanton, Susan B. Anthony, and Matilda J. Gage. Rochester, N.Y.: Charles Mann, 1881, 1882, 1886. Vol. 4 ed. Susan B. Anthony and Ida Husted Harper. Indianapolis: Hollenback Press, 1902. Vols. 5 and 6 ed. Ida Husted Harper. New York: J. J. Little & Ives, 1922.

Palmer, Phoebe. *Entire Devotion to God.* N.p., n.d. Reprint. Salem, Ohio: Schmul Publishers, n.d.

_____. *The Promise of the Father; or, A Neglected Specialty of the Last Days.* Boston: Henry V. Degen, 1859; reprint, Salem, Ohio: Schmul Publishers, n.d.

_____. *The Way of Holiness with Notes by the Way; Being a Narrative of Religious Experience Resulting from a Determination to be a Bible Christian.* New York: Piercy and Reed, 1843. Reprint. Salem, Ohio: Schmul Publishing, 1988.

Roberts, Benjamin T. *Ordaining Women.* Rochester, N.Y.: Earnest Christian Publishing House, 1891.

Shaw, S. B., ed. *Echoes of the General Holiness Assembly.* Chicago: Shaw Publishers, 1901.

Smith, Amanda Berry. *An Autobiography. The Story of the Lord's Dealings with Mrs. Amanda Smith the Colored Evangelist.* Introduction by J. M. Thoburn. Chicago: Meyer & Bro., 1893.

Smith, Hannah Whitall. *Religious Fanaticism: Extracts from the Papers of Hannah Whitall Smith.* Edited by Ray Strachey. London: Faber & Gwyer, 1928.

Smith, Sarah. *Life Sketches of Mother Sarah Smith.* Anderson, Ind.: Gospel Trumpet, [1902]. Reprint. Guthrie, Okla.: Faith Publishing House, n.d.

Stevens, Doris. *Jailed for Freedom: The Story of the Militant American Suffragist Movement.* New York: Boni and Liveright, 1920. Reprint. New York: Schocken Books, 1976.

Swarth, Helen. *My Life in a Commune.* N.p., n.d.

Vorn Holz, Miranda L. *The Old Paths.* Cincinnati: M. W. Knapp, [1898].

Wesley, John. *A Plain Account of Christian Perfection.* London, 1872. Reprint.
    Kansas City, Mo.: Beacon Hill Press of Kansas City, 1966.

Wheatley, Richard. *The Life and Letters of Mrs. Phoebe Palmer.* New York: W.
    C. Palmer, 1881. Reprint. New York: Garland Publishing, 1984.

White, Kent. *The Word of God Coming Again: Return of Apostolic Faith Church
    and Works Now Due.* Winton, Bournemouth, England: Apostolic Faith
    Church, 1919.

Wilson, Elizabeth. *A Scriptural View of Woman's Rights and Duties.* Philadel-
    phia: Wm. S. Young, 1849.

Articles and Pamphlets

"Bishop Says Her Heart Is Broken." *World,* 1922.

"Bishop v. Drink." *Time,* 18 December 1939, 40.

Booth, Catherine. *Female Ministry: Woman's Right to Preach the Gospel.* N.p.,
    1859. Reprint. New York: Salvation Army Supplies Printing and Pub-
    lishing Department, 1975.

Bowles, Ada C. "Woman in the Ministry." In *Woman's Work in America,* ed.
    Annie Nathan Miller, 206–17. New York: Henry Holt and Co., 1891.
    Reprint. New York: Arno Press, 1972.

Brody, Catharine. "Pastor-Husband Jealous Asserts Woman Bishop." *New
    York Globe,* 9 February 1921.

The Burning Bush. 5 January 1905; 16, 23, 30 November 1905; 18, 25 Janu-
    ary 1906; 15 February 1906; 1 March 1906.

"Cake Walk Chaos." *Daily Express* (London), 8 December 1904.

Casey, Lee. "Bishop White of Denver—A Cromwell in Skirts." *Denver Rocky
    Mountain News,* 28 June 1946, 14.

Cowan, John L. "Acrobatic Religionists: The Fantastic Faith of the Holy
    Jumpers—Some Account of the Origin, Growth, and Odd Practices of
    a Curious Western Cult." *Great Southwest Magazine,* June 1907, 66–67,
    82–83.

"The Dancers." *Star* (London), 6 December 1904.

"Dancing Delirium—Pentecostal Scenes at Camberwall—Four Hours of
    Acrobatic Revivalism" [1904]. Hannah Whitall Smith Papers, File
    "Pentecostal Dancers," Asbury Theological Seminary Archives, Asbury,
    Kentucky.

"Denver Catholic Register Historical Index 1913–1939." N.p., n.d.

"Denver Woman Who Is Creating Sensation in East." *Denver Times,* 29
    December 1902, 5.

"Exciting Revival." *Attleboro Sun,* 27 December 1902.

"Faith Dancers." *London Daily Chronicle,* 5 December 1904.

"Founder of Pillar of Fire Sect Denies any Part in KKK Threat." *Catholic
    Review Digest,* 10 March 1922.

"Fundamentalist Pillar." *Time,* 8 July 1946, 73–74.

Godbey, William B. "Experience of Dr. W. B. Godbey, Evangelist of Ken-
    tucky." *Guide to Holiness,* December 1896, 222–23.

_____. *Woman Preacher.* Atlanta: Office of the Way of Life, 1891.

"Hell and Damnation." *Attleboro Sun,* 24 December 1902.

"Holiness Revival Creating an Uproar: Mrs. Kent White of Denver Aston-
    ishes Attleboro, Mass. and Launches Heavenly Dynamite by Tongue
    and Pen." *Denver Post,* 29 December 1902, 7.

"Holy Dancers Hotly Assailed." *Morning Leader* (London), 7 December 1904.

"Holy Jiggery." *Star* (London), 6 December 1904.

"The Holy Jumpers—Another New Religion." Photocopy without name of
    newspaper, n.d.

Irwin, Inez Haynes. "The Equal Rights Amendment: Why the Woman's
    Party Is for It." *Good Housekeeping,* March 1924, 18, 158–61.

Journal Kentucky Conference Methodist Episcopal Church, South, 1921, 72–73.

*Journal of the Thirty-second Session of the Colorado Annual Conference of the Method-
    ist Episcopal Church Held at Boulder, Colorado, June 7 to 11, 1894.* Denver:
    Dove Printer, 1894.

"'Jumpers' Jumped and Judge Thomas Lectured." *Denver Post,* 9 February
    1903, 2

"'Jumpers' of Denver." *Washington Post,* 25 August 1907.

"Jumpers Jailed for Street Disturbance." *Denver Republic,* 9 February 1903,
    10.

"'Jumpers' Queer Rites." *Denver Times,* 27 July 1902, 10.

"Jumpers Say Askew Met with the Wrath of God." *Denver Post,* 9 January
    1904, 2.

Kenton, Edna. "The Ladies' Next Step: The Case for the Equal Rights
    Amendment." *Harper's Magazine,* February 1926, 366–74.

"Ku Klux Klan Letter of Warning Sent to Register." *Denver Catholic Register,* 9
    March 1922, 1.

"The Light Fantastic." *News of the World* (London), 4 December 1904.

Lutz, Alma. "Shall Women's Work Be Regulated by Law?" *Atlantic Monthly,*
    September 1930, 321–27.

"Makes Violent Attack on Priests, Sisters, Knights of Columbus." *Catholic
    Review Digest,* 1 February 1923.

"May Women Preach?" *Quarterly Review of the Methodist Episcopal Church,
    South,* n.s. 3 (July 1881): 478–88.

"Memoirs—Rev. W. B. Godbey, D.D." *Journal Kentucky Conference Methodist
    Episcopal Church, South 1921.*

Merthyr Express (London), 25 March 1905.

*Minutes of the Fifty-Eighth Session of the Kentucky Annual Conference of the Method-
    ist Episcopal Church, South Held in Shelbyville, Ky., September 18–25, 1878.*
    Louisville: John P. Morton and Co., 1878.

*Minutes of the Fifty-Ninth Session of the Kentucky Annual Conference of the Method-
    ist Episcopal Church, South Held in Richmond, Ky., September 17–23, 1879.*
    Louisville: John P. Morton and Co., 1879.

*Minutes of the Fifty-Seventh Session of the Kentucky Annual Conference of the Meth-
    odist Episcopal Church, South Held in Winchester, Ky., September 5–12, 1877.*
    Louisville: John P. Morton and Co., 1877.

Minutes of the Fifty-Sixth Session of the Kentucky Annual Conference of the Methodist Episcopal Church, South Held in Nicholasville, Ky., September 13–19, 1876. Louisville: John P. Morton and Co., 1876.

"Monthly Review: The Home Field." *Guide to Holiness,* November 1895, 158.

"Needless Violence." *Daily Mirror* (London), 9 December 1904.

"Neighbors Say Worship Is Too Loud." *Denver Republican,* 5 August 1908, 11.

"Pentecostal Dancers." *Daily Mail* (London), 2 December 1904.

"Pentecostal Dancers at Dowlais." Photocopy without name of newspaper, n.d.

"Pillar." *American Magazine,* May 1937, 101.

"Pillar of Fire Dry Legion Acts Out Evils of Liquor in Brooklyn Church Pulpit." *Life,* 29 January 1940, 42–43.

"Pillar of Fire Head Examined at Trial." *Denver Rocky Mountain News,* 17 February 1922, 14.

Pool, Lillian. "Experience and Call to the Ministry." In *Women Preachers,* ed. Fanny McDowell Hunter. Dallas: Berachah Printing, 1905.

"Prayer and Faith Alleged to Have Restored a Woman's Sight—Hundreds Give up their All under Spur of Religious Fervor." *Denver Post,* 5 August 1902, 1.

"Rev. Kent White." *Denver Rocky Mountain News,* 2 August 1940, 13.

"Riot in Church Leads to Arrest of 4 Persons." *Salt Lake Telegraph,* 11 April 1904.

Rocky Mountain Pillar of Fire, 15 February 1905, 10.

"Self-Named Woman Bishop Violent in Anti-Catholicity." *Denver Catholic Register,* 1 February 1923, 1.

"12,000 of Klan out at Jersey Meeting," *New York Times,* 3 May 1923, 1.

Willing, Jennie Fowler. "Every Woman a Missionary." *Guide to Holiness,* November 1896, 178–79.

———. "God's Great Women: Eve." *Guide to Holiness,* January 1897, 28–29, 32.

———. "God's Great Women: God's Modern Woman." *Guide to Holiness,* December 1897, 226–27.

"Woman Bishop to Conduct Services in Manitou Now." *Colorado Springs Gazette,* July 1922.

"Women Preachers." *Woman Citizen,* December 1920, 794–96, 802.

SECONDARY SOURCES

Books

Ahlstrom, Sydney E. *A Religious History of the American People.* New Haven: Yale University Press, 1972.

Becker, Susan D. *The Origins of the Equal Rights Amendment: American Feminism between the Wars.* Westport, Conn.: Greenwood Press, 1981.

Blee, Kathleen M. *Women of the Klan.* Berkeley and Los Angeles: University of California Press, 1991.

Brereton, Virginia Lieson. *From Sin to Salvation: Stories of Women's Conversions, 1800 to the Present.* Bloomington: Indiana University Press, 1991.

Brown, Dorothy M. *Setting a Course: American Women in the 1920s.* Boston: Twayne Publishers, 1987.

Chalmers, David M. *Hooded Americanism: The First Century of the Ku Klux Klan 1865–1965.* Garden City, N.Y.: Doubleday, 1965.

Cott, Nancy F. *The Bonds of Womanhood: "Woman's Sphere" in New England, 1780–1835.* New Haven: Yale University Press, 1977.

_____. *The Grounding of Modern Feminism.* New Haven: Yale University Press, 1987.

Coulter, Merton. *The Civil War and Readjustment in Kentucky.* Gloucester, Mass.: Peter Smith, 1966.

Davis, Lenwood G., and Janet L. Sims-Wood, comps. *The Ku Klux Klan: A Bibliography.* Westport, Conn.: Greenwood Press, 1984.

Dayton, Donald W. *Theological Roots of Pentecostalism.* Grand Rapids: Francis Asbury Press of Zondervan Publishing House, 1987.

DeBerg, Betty A. *Ungodly Women: Gender and the First Wave of American Fundamentalism.* Philadelphia: Augsburg/Fortress, 1990.

Dieter, Melvin Easterday. *The Holiness Revival of the Nineteenth Century.* Studies in Evangelism, no. 1. Metuchen, N.J.: Scarecrow Press, 1980.

Ferguson, Charles W. *The Confusion of Tongues.* Garden City, N.Y.: Doubleday, Doran & Co., 1928.

Goldberg, Robert Alan. *Hooded Empire: The Ku Klux Klan in Colorado.* Urbana: University of Illinois Press, 1981.

Heilbrun, Carolyn G. *Writing a Woman's Life.* New York: Ballantine Books, 1988.

Higham, John. *Strangers in the Land: Patterns of American Nativism, 1860–1925.* New York: Atheneum, 1963.

Hill, Mary A. *Charlotte Perkins Gilman: The Making of a Radical Feminist, 1860–1896.* Philadelphia: Temple University Press, 1980.

Hudson, Winthrop. *Religion in America.* 4th ed. New York: Macmillan, 1987.

Hutchison, William R. *Modernist Impulse in American Protestantism.* Oxford: Oxford University Press, 1976.

Jackson, Kenneth T. *The Ku Klux Klan in the City: 1915–1930.* New York: Oxford University Press, 1967.

Johnson, Charles A. *The Frontier Camp Meeting: Religion's Harvest Time.* Dallas: Southern Methodist University Press, 1955.

Jones, Charles E. *A Guide to the Study of the Holiness Movement.* ATLA Bibliography Series, no. 1. Metuchen, N.J.: Scarecrow Press, 1974.

_____. *Perfectionist Persuasion: The Holiness Movement and American Methodism, 1867–1936.* ATLA Monograph Series, no. 5. Metuchen, N.J.: Scarecrow Press, 1974.

Jones, Maldwyn Allen. *American Immigration.* Chicago: University of Chicago Press, 1960.

Kraditor, Aileen S., ed. *Up From the Pedestal: Selected Writings in the History of American Feminism.* Chicago: Quadrangle Books, 1968.

Lemons, J. Stanley. *The Woman Citizen: Social Feminism in the 1920's.* Urbana: University of Illinois Press, 1973.

McLoughlin, William G. *Revivals, Awakenings, and Reform: An Essay on Religion and Social Change in America, 1607–1977.* Chicago History of American Religion. Chicago: University of Chicago Press, 1978.

Magnuson, Norris. *Salvation in the Slums.* ATLA Monograph Series, no. 10. Metuchen, N.J.: Scarecrow Press, 1977.

Marsden, George. *Fundamentalism and American Culture: The Shaping of Twentieth-Century Evangelicalism 1870–1925.* Oxford: Oxford University Press, 1980.

Marty, Martin E. *Modern American Religion.* Vol. 1, *The Irony of It All 1893–1919.* Chicago: University of Chicago Press, 1986.

Miller, Adam W. *An Introduction to the New Testament.* Anderson, Ind.: Warner Press, 1946.

Numbers, Ronald L. *Prophetess of Health: A Study of Ellen G. White.* York: Harper & Row, 1976.

O'Neill, William L. *Everyone Was Brave: A History of Feminism in America.* New York: Quadrangle/New York Times Book Co., 1969.

Peters, John Leland. *Christian Perfection and American Methodism.* New York: Abingdon Press, 1956.

Porterfield, Amanda. *Feminine Spirituality in America: From Sarah Edwards to Martha Graham.* Philadelphia: Temple University Press, 1980.

Raser, Harold E. *Phoebe Palmer: Her Life and Thought.* Lewiston, N.Y.: Edwin Mellon Press, 1987.

Rothman, Sheila M. *Woman's Proper Place: A History of Changing Ideals and Practices, 1870 to the Present.* New York: Basic Books, 1978.

Ryan, Mary P. *Womanhood in America from Colonial Times to the Present.* New York: New Viewpoints, 1979.

Schmidt, Jean Miller. *Souls or the Social Order: The Two-Party System in American Protestantism.* Brooklyn, N.Y.: Carlson Publishing, 1991.

Smith, John W. V. *The Quest for Holiness and Unity.* Anderson, Ind.: Warner Press, 1980.

Smith, Timothy L. *Called unto Holiness: The Story of the Nazarenes: The Formative Years.* Kansas City, Mo.: Nazarene Publishing House, 1962.

_____. *Revivalism and Social Reform in Mid-Nineteenth Century America.* New York: Abingdon Press, 1957; reprint with new title *Revivalism and Social Reform: American Protestantism on the Eve of the Civil War.* Baltimore: Johns Hopkins University Press, 1980.

Sweet, Leonard I. *The Minister's Wife: Her Role in Nineteenth-Century American Evangelism.* Philadelphia: Temple University Press, 1983.

Synan, Vinson. *The Holiness-Pentecostal Movement in the United States.* Grand Rapids, Mich.: William B. Eerdmans Publishing, 1971.

Szasz, Ferenc Morton. *The Divided Mind of Protestant America, 1880–1930.* University: University of Alabama Press, 1982.

Tucker, Cynthia Grant. *Prophetic Sisterhood: Liberal Women Ministers of the Frontier, 1880–1930.* Beacon Press, 1990.

Ware, Susan. *Beyond Suffrage: Women in the New Deal.* Cambridge: Harvard University Press, 1981.

_____. *Holding Their Own: American Women in the 1930s.* Boston: Twayne Publishers, 1982.

Weber, Timothy. *Living in the Shadow of the Second Coming: American Premillennialism 1875–1982.* New York: Oxford University Press, 1979. Enl. ed. Grand Rapids, Mich: Zondervan, 1983.

White, Charles Edward. *Beauty of Holiness.* Grand Rapids, Mich.: Francis Asbury Press of Zondervan Publishing House, 1986.

Williams, Michael. *The Shadow of the Pope.* New York: McGraw Hill, 1932.

Wyman, David S. *The Abandonment of the Jews: America and the Holocaust, 1941–1945.* New York: Pantheon Books, 1984.

_____. *Paper Walls: America and the Refugee Crisis 1938–1941.* Amherst: University of Massachusetts Press, 1968.

Articles

Bainbridge, William Sims, and Rodney Stark. "Sectarian Tension." *Review of Religious Research,* December 1980, 105–23.

Bendroth, Margaret Lamberts. "Fundamentalism and Femininity: Points of Encounter Between Religious Conservatives and Women, 1919–1935." *Church History* 61 (June 1992): 221–33.

Bennett, Adrian A. "Doing More Than They Intended." In *Women in New Worlds.* Vol. 2, ed. Rosemary Skinner Keller, Louise L. Queen, and Hilah F. Thomas, 249–67. Nashville: Abingdon Press, 1982.

Dayton, Donald W., and Lucille Sider Dayton. "Recovering a Heritage: Part II, Evangelical Feminism." *Post American,* August–September 1974, 7–9.

Gordon, Linda. "Voluntary Motherhood: The Beginnings of Feminist Birth Control Ideas in Nineteenth-Century United States." In *Clio's Consciousness Raised,* ed. Mary S. Hartman and Lois Banner, 54–71. New York: Octagon Books, 1976.

Hardesty, Nancy, Lucille Sider Dayton, and Donald W. Dayton. "Women in the Holiness Movement: Feminism in the Evangelical Tradition." In *Women of Spirit: Female Leadership in the Jewish and Christian Traditions,* ed. Rosemary Ruether and Eleanor McLaughlin, 225–54. New York: Simon and Schuster, 1979.

Hay, John F. "The Book of Jonah: The Missing Witness." *God's Revivalist and Bible Advocate,* January 1991, 14–15.

Howard, Ivan. "Wesley vs. Phoebe Palmer: An Extended Controversy." *Wesleyan Theological Journal* 11 (Spring 1971): 31–40.

Jacquet, Constant H., Jr., *Women Ministers in 1986 and 1977: A Ten Year View.* New York: Office of Research and Evaluation, National Council of Churches, 1988.

Johnson, Benton. "On Church and Sect." *American Sociological Review* 28 (August 1963): 539–49.

Kallman, Harmon. "Pillar of Fire Church History Linked to That of Founder's Family." *Denver Post,* 20 August 1955, 5.

Kenneally, James J. "Eve, Mary and the Historians: American Catholicism and Women." *Horizons* 3 (1976): 187–202.

Loveland, Anne C. "Domesticity and Religion in the Antebellum Period: The Career of Phoebe Palmer." *Historian,* May 1977, 455–71.

Miller, Robert M. "A Note on the Relationship between the Protestant Churches and the Revised Ku Klux Klan." *Journal of Southern History* 22 (August 1956): 355–68.

Stanley, Susie C. "Empowered Foremothers: Wesleyan/Holiness Women Speak to Today's Christian Feminists." *Wesleyan Theological Journal,* 1989:103–16.

Welter, Barbara. "She Hath Done What She Could: Protestant Women's Missionary Careers in Nineteenth-Century America." In *Women in American Religion,* ed. Janet Wilson James, 111–25. Philadelphia: University of Pennsylvania Press, 1980.

Unpublished Materials

Brown, Joanne Elizabeth C. "Jennie Fowler Willing (1834–1916): Methodist Churchwoman and Reformer." Ph.D. diss., Boston University Graduate School, 1983.

Brown, Kenneth O. "Leadership in the National Holiness Association with Special Reference to Eschatology, 1867–1919." Ph.D. diss., Drew University, 1988.

Davis, James H. "The Rise of the Ku Klux Klan in Colorado, 1921–1925." Master's thesis, University of Denver, 1963.

Dayton, Donald W. "Evangelical Roots of Feminism." N.p., n.d. (Mimeographed.)

_____. "Prophesying Daughters: The Ministry of Women in the Holiness Movement." Paper presented at the United Methodist Church Conference "Women in New Worlds." Cincinnati, 1980. (Mimeographed.)

Gaddis, Merrill Elmer. "Christian Perfectionism in America." Ph.D. diss., University of Chicago, 1929.

Gooderham, George E. "The Pillar of Fire. 1934." In *Denver Cults: 1934–1937,* ed. William Henry Bernhardt, 159–93. Denver: n.p., 1937.

Hardesty, Nancy A. "'Your Daughters Shall Prophesy': Revivalism and Feminism in the Age of Finney." Ph.D. diss., University of Chicago, 1976.

Ingersol, Robert Stanley. "Burden of Dissent: Mary Lee Cagle and the Southern Holiness Movement." Ph.D. diss., Duke University, 1989.

Nelson, Douglas J. "For Such a Time as This: The Story of Bishop William J. Seymour and the Azusa Street Revival: A Search for Pentecostal Charismatic Roots." Ph.D. diss., University of Birmingham, 1981.

Nelson, Marjory. "Ladies in the Streets: A Sociological Analysis of the National Woman's Party, 1910–1930." Ph.D. diss., State University of New York at Buffalo, 1976.

Index